The Plot Against Humanity

The Plot Against

Humanity

SCOTT HOWARD

Author of *The Transgender-Industrial Complex*
and *The Open Society Playbook*

ANTELOPE HILL PUBLISHING

Cover art by Swifty. Photo credits to Stable Diffusion Demo.
Edited and formatted by Margaret Bauer.

The author can be contacted at:
Scott2hotthoward@protonmail.com

Antelope Hill Publishing
www.antelopehillpublishing.com

Paperback ISBN-13: 978-1-956887-51-8
EPUB ISBN-13: 978-1-956887-52-5

"Life is encrypted, you are modified
Like a virus in a lullaby
Artificial 'til the day you die, silly programme
You're corrupted"
– Bring Me the Horizon, "Kingslayer"

"So we just went ahead and fixed the glitch."
– Bob Slydell, *Office Space*

Contents

Introduction

The year 2020 saw a sea change in the way the world we once knew functioned. As both catalyst and accelerant, the COVID-19 pandemic brought the easy button era of neo-liberalism to a screeching halt. Borders closed, paranoia spiked, and as these traumatic events always seem to provide justification for, civil liberties disappeared and surveillance increased—for your safety of course. To be fair, as events in places like New York and Milan unfolded, COVID-19 had all the appearances of another Spanish Flu with a death toll in the millions. Certain restrictions and an abundance of caution were a rational and intelligent response. But once "peaceful protesters" were allowed to gather freely in the wake of the demise of one George Floyd, it became glaringly obvious that it was not as it seemed. It never is in the Propaganda Age.

Much like "my body my choice" when it comes to sacrificing the unborn to Moloch but not when it comes to coerced injections—the contradictions on full display after the 2022 Supreme Court ruling on *Roe v. Wade* for example—anyone with eyes to see observed that reality and narrative were at odds. Why would thousands be allowed to stand shoulder-to-shoulder for the right to burn down your local Walgreens in the name of racial justice, if we were really concerned with stopping the spread of a deadly virus? And why did it just so happen that the Floyd incident became the media's fixation right when the people seemed likely to band together over frustration with their governments' (mis-)management of the virus on top of massive economic changes skewing once again to the benefit of Wall Street and high finance?

A large-scale popular movement that discarded division in favor of demanding a genuinely equitable and sustainable system is the last thing the Establishment wanted (and wants), and so just like the crisis of Occupy Wall Street was averted with the sowing of discord through all sorts of racial grievances, so, too, was this one. A whole bunch of climate and sexuality and gender grievances were thrown in for good measure, but what we can see in the rhetoric is that it aims to take the moral high ground through cooption of terms and concepts, but always in inverse relationship to the reality. If the reader has ever seen the "you owe that man your cookie" meme, that is in essence what we're talking about here: some ghoul from Goldman Sachs weaponizing racial grievances against the working class in the name of "equality" to maintain control and destroy the ability for any self-sufficiency outside or collective action against their system.

Why should we take issue with the world they've created, though? Aren't even the poor today in most cases far better off in material comfort than at any other time in human history? Well, yes, but the materiality is actually the crux of it—there is nothing at its center of any true value. It is amoral at best, immoral at worst. So, we get our bread and circuses and fight each other while the system's architects laugh all the way to the bank to make that money machine go BRRRR! To quote The Acacia Strain, "This is a Lifetime movie on a global scale." The melodrama is nauseating. January 6th: Very Scary. Glows in the dark, too, I might add.

We are, without question, on the cusp of a Brave New World, turned upside-down by the forces unleased on the back of the COVID-19 pandemic. Whether the virus was intentionally released or the powers that be simply did not want a good crisis to go to waste is at this juncture irrelevant; what is of the utmost importance is where we are being led, by whom, and why. The virus has proven to be the justification for catalyzing certain things and accelerating others that have been building quietly in the shadows—though not altogether hiding—for some time. An unholy alliance— with much overlap—of technocrats, eugenicists, collectivists, occultists, deviants, and transhumanists form the nucleus of what deigns to be the permanent ruling class of humanity, provided they don't precipitate the demise of the species as we know it or altogether. That this nucleus is comprised of a massively-outsized, in proportion to the population, contingent of Jews is the truth of the matter that accusations of "anti-Semitism" as always seek to obscure. The treatment of the artist formerly known as Kanye West for having the audacity to observe something similar in his dealings with corrupt record executives, businessmen, and lawyers leading to a collusive cancellation—spearheaded by these very-same Jews and their compatriots—is illustrative of how this soft power is maintained. Cancel culture is the neo-Maoist product of these influences.

These facts are inconvenient for the narrative that's been constructed, but they *are* facts. They will be exhibited throughout this book to provide the reader with a clear picture of the situation as it truly is, *not* as it is presented. Through an intensive indoctrination effort, censorship, technological surveillance and alteration of behaviors, and rigid policing of the Overton Window, most people have been heavily-conditioned into a preset belief structure that prevents them from considering that which might be contrary to the almighty Narrative, or else funnels them into irrelevant and/or harmful conflicts that only serve to reinforce the dialectic. This was something West noted—and was naturally lambasted for by the media—regarding the suspicious demise of Floyd and the weaponization of the Black Lives Matter "movement" in spearheading what he calls the "trauma economy."

Our entry point in exploring this network of control and its aims will be the deep interconnections of the COVID establishment with governments, universities, well-funded non-governmental organizations (NGOs), and private corporations and high finance, including entities that are enabling governments dedicated to surveillance of citizens and enforced conformity in attitudes and behavior. These trends are increasingly apparent throughout the West and are particularly welcomed by the political left. Quite clearly, the COVID crisis is seen by such "elites" as a golden opportunity to ratchet up control and conformity in not just Western societies, but across the entire globe. Although it remains an open question as to whether it will be one continuous global bloc, two or more competing factions, or some other scenario, in any of the pre-planned cases the outcome will result in a complete loss of privacy, individuality, meaning, and quite possibly our very humanity.

There are multiple avenues by which this outcome might occur, ranging from massive global conflict and upheaval, making what for many people would be otherwise-unpalatable alternatives of transhumanism suddenly appear all right by comparison, to the slow slouch to a dopamine-hit-addicted slug race of the future. No matter, we are promised this future will be glorious and utopian. Despite the looming climate apocalypse we keep hearing about, the "elites" nevertheless promise to have turned earth into an Edenic paradise by the year 2030—the year their Messiah, FM-2030, will be reincarnated. Joking aside, FM-2030 was a real person, and the year 2030 clearly has deep significance.

Regarding the man FM-2030, his real name was Fereidoun M. Esfandiary. He was a transhumanist who served on the United Nations Conciliation Commission for Palestine and was a corporate consultant for JC Penny and Lockheed. He chose the name FM-2030 as he believed he would celebrate his hundredth birthday in 2030 (at present, his corpse is being cryopreserved at the Alcor Life Extension Foundation facility in Arizona) and because, as he stated, "Conventional names define a person's past: ancestry, ethnicity, nationality, religion. . . . The name 2030 reflects my conviction that the years around 2030 will be a magical time. . . . In 2030 we will be ageless and everyone will have an excellent chance to live forever."[1] Notice that you will also have erased ancestry, ethnicity, nationality, and religion.

Not stopping there, FM-2030 believed that the next evolution of humanity would be as "post-biological organisms" that had moved beyond their bodily limitations through technology. The universality of this new epoch is utopian in the literal translation of utopia: no place. Consider one of the most celebrated songs by the squishy managerial class today, a sort of international anthem, "Imagine" by John Lennon:

> *Imagine there's no heaven*   *Livin' for today*
> *It's easy if you try*   *Imagine there's no countries*
> *No hell below us*   *It isn't hard to do*
> *Above us, only sky*   *Nothing to kill or die for*
> *Imagine all the people*   *And no religion, too*

Presented as a good thing, of course. No identity to speak of, no meaning, only ever living for the now of whatever fleeting pleasures are allowed to you.

Transhumanism *is* a religion, though, a perverse and false one, certainly, but one of many of its kind to take form in the otherwise terribly sterile world of secular humanism. We are all familiar with the dogmas and mantras of the mainstream religion of scientism unleashed on the globe through COVID-19 like a shaken hornets' nest of jihadis loosed from medieval Arabia. Trust the science, as it were. Have faith in the high priests in lab coats telling

---

[1] Quoted in Schnall, interview.

you to inject whatever mystery substance they've concocted. Do not question the narrative, and submit, wholly, to what the omnipresent screens demand. If you enjoyed the punting on civil liberties, the destruction of non-mega-corporation businesses, and the forcible subjection of people to ill-defined experimental gene therapies that kicked off the new Roaring Twenties, then to you the future's so bright you gotta wear shades, man. Whether it's a Pfizer concoction masquerading as a vaccine or the chemical castration of a child, either way that's the bright rainbow of Progress.

Curious that Progress looks a whole lot like feudalism but with a smartphone, though. The "elites" are tired of having citizens and they want subjects again—"let them eat bugs" as it were. They want us to be like serfs of yore with bi-annual trips to the lord's manor for an injection, quite possibly used as literal human resources if they don't ultimately try to jettison us as dead weight altogether. They refuse to be held to account. Everything is done specifically to distract and detract, and keep your eyes everywhere but where they should be.

Think about mass Third World immigration into the West as an example. It is of course about ideology, voting tendencies, and acquiring cheap labor, but it also serves the purpose of fracturing social cohesion and the ability to organize and resist. It creates tribalism and hostilities, and it's compounded dramatically by the propaganda and the constant attempts by federal "law enforcement" to goad the mentally ill into some kind of mass shooting or terror attack. It's the same reason the agencies and governments have aided and abetted jihadi Islam in the West: it sows fear and resentment—to say nothing of the Zionist dialectic it reinforces.

The precipitous decline in standards of all kinds across the board in the West is directly attributable to decisions undertaken consciously to completely re-shape our environs; the resulting decrepitude is not as a result of naivete or stupidity, it is the result of a coterie in control acting explicitly on behalf of their vision of what the future should look like. It does not include free and independent peoples and cultures—it does not, in the least, include *people* as we understand the word at all—and it certainly does not include faith but that in the machine.

At the end of my first book, *The Transgender-Industrial Complex*, I intentionally broadened out the scope to illustrate that despite the indoctrination we are subjected to in order to make us ever-more specialized and more generally useless, the "masters of mankind" are not siloed; their project is all-encompassing, and transgenderism is but one aspect of the efforts to completely re-make (or un-make as the case may be) humanity. Whether it's computer engineers or social engineers, there is an overarching belief that if we can just build the right system, then we can finally have it all. It is the utopian terrestrial dream that's really little more than a delusion, the same as it ever was. The ruling class is rabid in its faith of transhumanism, and possessed with their religious fervor, they aim to convert the whole globe by whatever means necessary.

In my second book, *The Open Society Playbook*, I diagrammed exactly how the power structure "opens up" a society to feminism, mass immigration, LGBTQ "rights," and everything else we recognize as destructive to the fabric of a healthy, functioning society. The open society is permissive of everything antithetical to its former core values and people, wearing a smiley face as it stabs you in the back. This is one of the central features of the era of neo-liberalism, with its soft comforts along the march to atomization. More stuff, less meaning, and a constant slow grinding away of both individual *and* community—and especially of the family. It's how the West got to the inflection point of 2020 and why it's proven largely unable to mount any appreciable resistance to the abuses to which we have been continually subjected. If you do not understand what is good, then you cannot understand what is evil, especially if evil is wearing kid gloves. Atomized and terrified, such a population is mighty easy to control—and if it believes the highest virtue is supporting the very things destroying it, so much the better.

Though not entirely uniform in that there are subsets within the Establishment jockeying for position as ultimate hegemons with sometimes competing visions, the general thrust remains uniform in its support for the noxious policies that have been so central to neo-liberalism, from open borders to the erosion of civil liberties to vast amounts of wealth accruing in increasingly-few hands. For the transhumanists, as globalism becomes lockdowns, social credit scores, and mandatory "vaccines" for COVID-19, the reader would do well to remember that those hands are the architects of this system, and the obvious beneficiaries; the only real disagreements are how they will allocate power to themselves, who will occupy the very top, and what form humanity itself will take. It has been a long and step-by-step process, and the role of creating an "open society" with fertile ground for what comes next is an essential step in the agenda for its implementation in the West and across the globe.

The purpose of this book is not to be a postmortem of the West, as this has been done extensively elsewhere, and if you are reading this, you very likely understand that the previous era—neo-liberalism—is now rapidly coming to an end, giving way to the transhumanist-informed, bio-digital age. Through various intersecting ideologies and their applications, we are being directed into a bio-digital hive. If this all sounds rather conspiratorial, well—it is. But not all conspiracies are mere "theories" or wild fiction. This book will show just that.

In Chapter One, we will look at the ideology/religion that is transhumanism and what its acolytes believe in greater detail. In Chapter Two, we will look more closely at the World Economic Forum (WEF) and its founder and Executive Chairman Klaus Schwab—a leading figure for the implementation of the Internet of Things, the Fourth Industrial Revolution, and the Great Reset. The World Economic Forum is sort of like the mother of all NGOs and states that its mission is to "improv[e] the state of the world by engaging business, political, academic, and other leaders of society *to shape global, regional, and industry agendas*."[2] The terms Internet of Things (IoT), the Fourth Industrial Revolution, and the Great Reset are all concepts owing their genesis or popularization to Schwab and the World Economic Forum. The IoT is, according to Alexander S. Gillis, "a system of interrelated computing devices, mechanical and digital machines, objects, animals or people that are provided with unique identifiers (UIDs) and the ability to transfer data over a network without requiring human-to-human or human-to-computer interaction." The Fourth Industrial Revolution is, for Devon McGinnis of Salesforce, "a way of describing the blurring of boundaries between the physical, digital, and biological worlds. It's a fusion of advances in artificial intelligence (AI), robotics, the Internet of Things (IoT), 3D printing, genetic engineering, quantum computing, and other technologies," including blockchain. Finally, the Great Reset is a WEF initiative launched in June 2020 capitalizing on the COVID-19 pandemic that explicitly links "recovery" from the pandemic with the various constituent parts of the Fourth Industrial Revolution; for Schwab, "the world must act jointly and swiftly to revamp all aspects of our societies and economies, from education to social contracts and working conditions. Every country, from the United States to China, must participate, and every industry, from oil and gas to tech, must be transformed. In short, we need a 'Great Reset' of capitalism."[3]

---

[2] Via their website. Emphasis Added.
[3] Schwab, "Now Is the Time."

Chapter Three will delve into the cult of scientism and how COVID-19 is being used to usher in the Great Reset, as Schwab states that, "The pandemic represents a rare but narrow window of opportunity to reflect, reimagine, and reset our world."[4] For Schwab, speaking in the context of the WEF-supported Cyber Polygon exercise, via their website, "The pandemic has changed the world, and one of the most striking transformations [one which elsewhere Schwab describes as 'exciting'] has been the complete digitization of all aspects of our lives." The core of this digitization is centered on artificial intelligence, which Chapter Four will explicate and explain the ramifications of. In Chapter Five, we'll take the *Open Society* approach to diagnosing how crises are and will continue to be manufactured in order to get people to voluntarily sign up for the Great Reset or else essentially leave them little choice but to do so. Chapter Six will explore the ways in which finance has proven to be the ultimate leverage tool and how without a complete reconfiguration—a reset if you like—we will never be able to escape from the clutches of the "elites" and where they want to force us, which is not a happy place if you value meaning and what makes you, well, you.

---

[4] Ibid.

Chapter One:
Transhumans and Vampires

"Posthumans will be almost entirely augmented—human minds in artificial, eternally upgradable bodies. . . . Human nature is at a crossroads. In the coming decades we will experience a radical upgrading. . . . Genetic engineering, biotechnology, nanorobotics (microscopic robots inside the body) will bit by bit replace the fully biological body."

– Natasha Vita-More, Humanity+ Executive Director

"There has been a distinct warming up to human-less, contactless technology. Humans are biohazards, machines are not."

– Anuja Sonalker, founder and CEO of STEER Tech

These transhumanist technocrats are working to change our world completely and irrevocably for their own twisted purposes. Beyond their obvious motivations of limitless power and control, it is a story as old as man: the desire to taste the forbidden fruit, to cheat death, to engage in alchemical transmutation.

We already live in a world given to alchemy—and not just financial alchemy as George Soros's 1986 book title references, though it is curious that those powering the global order feel compelled to place references and symbols alluding to their motives in plain sight. These are very often esoteric and occultic in nature, if not demonic. Consider that alchemy is the act of transforming "base metals" into "noble metals"—although the transformations in our case here almost exclusively turn us away from nobility and toward debasement. Some transgender persons, for example, explicitly identify themselves with Baphomet, a goat-headed demon with both male and female anatomy. Baphomet has been adopted as a symbol by many esoteric belief systems as representing the Left-Hand Path of black magic.

The goat head is often seen in conjunction with a pentagram; the 2030 of "elite" obsession is also 2+3=5—five points or pentagram. Though this may be a stretch, and may be eminently silly to the reader, rest assured that a great many of the "elites" *actually believe* in things like astrology and numerology, and are deeply invested in the occult. Why do you think the powerful individuals who attend the bizarre rituals in places like Bohemian Grove and give praise to Moloch while sacrificing an effigy of a child do what they do? Moloch, for the record, was a Canaanite god associated with child sacrifice, through fire or war. "You shall not give any of your children to devote them by fire to Moloch, and so profane the name of your God" (Leviticus 18:21). Why do you think the LGBTQ agenda chooses to call itself Pride—a sin—and has adopted the rainbow, the symbol of God's covenant with Noah and his sons in Genesis to never again bring floodwaters forth as punishment?

As transhumanism asks, who needs God, though, when you have science? Transhumanism is the ideology-*cum*-religion motivating the leading faction of self-styled "masters of mankind" driving the Great Reset largely from the shadows. The global transhumanist organization Humanity+ defines it as the drive to eliminate aging and expand human capabilities, with technology used to "move beyond what some would think of as 'human.'" Humanity+ Executive Director Natasha Vita-More states that transhumanism has "become a worldview that represents the currents in global society."[5] This is absolutely true, particularly as the medical tyranny of 2020 opened the doors to all sorts of possibilities for the ruling class. Despite the fact that Vita-More's "Transhumanist Manifesto" declares that "each person deserves the right of genetic liberty," the majority of the ruling class does not agree when it comes to those outside the in-group. Relying on science and technology to improve human life is one thing, but using it to augment or modify it in a fundamentally transformative nature is quite another—especially when this is being done against our will.

Most people probably would not want to sacrifice their humanity, but to be fair, people like More who speak so plainly about their motivations

---

[5] Knoepfler, "Global transhumanism leader Natasha."

publicly are rather scarce. In the same way that corporations won't explicate the real economic reasons for their support for abortions on demand, trans-humans generally do not simply state that "we're going to fundamentally transform you whether you like it or not because [fill in the blank]." They need to maneuver you into such a place where it can happen without your knowing or without appreciable resistance. Relative ease of living is excellent for wearing down self-sufficiency and for getting most people to quietly look the other way while all kinds of immorality proliferate around them, but to trigger a more fundamental shift in how we live and who we are, that comfort has to be threatened.

For example, the World Economic Forum-supported Cyber Polygon simulated a cyberattack with participants responding to "a targeted supply chain attack on a corporate ecosystem in real time." Note the use of linkage here with words like ecosystem and the fact that the WEF notes, "A cyber attack with COVID-like characteristics would spread faster and farther than any biological virus. Its reproductive rate would be around 10 times greater than what we've experienced with the coronavirus."[6] It is, of course, merely kooky "conspiracy theory" to note that dry runs have been happening with alarming regularity already, because *none of this is at all scripted*. Right. The shortages, droughts, energy depot and food processing plant fires, and "existential crises" over *carbon emissions* are in no way manufactured. The media doesn't manufacture a moral panic every five minutes, and you should probably ignore the fact that meat is being phased-out because of cow farts in the pursuit of "net zero carbon emissions," while JBS Foods, the world's largest meatpacking company, not only partnered with the World Economic Forum in April 2021 to tackle "climate change" and acquired Vivera, Europe's third-largest "plant-based food" company that same month, but was suddenly and mysteriously assailed by ransomware the following month. How about fossil fuels and the Colonial Pipeline attack? The Pimpri-Chinchwad Smart City project in India? "IoT manufacturer" Sierra Wireless? Global wholesale distributor JBI? What about World Economic Forum partner Royal Dutch Shell, whose Emily Tan wrote for the WEF in February 2021 that "Never has there been a moment where businesses, energy consumers and governments—from Canada to China— are aligning on a common vision like this: a road to net-zero emissions"? For Tan, "Countries, governments and companies are aligning on a need

---

[6] World Economic Forum, "A cyber-attack with COVID-like characteristics?"

for net-zero—and this is an opportunity to rethink decarbonizing our cities." This term "decarbonizing" has been echoed by numerous Establishment figures, including that of Jewish US Secretary of the Treasury Janet Yellen, who in the midst of runaway inflation was only concerned with "decarbonizing the economy." I think we should de-Yellenize the economy, but I digress.

We see the connecting of the biological and digital spheres in Cyber Polygon, with the idea that "a secure approach to digital development today will determine the future of humanity for decades to come." For Schwab, "We need vaccines to immunize ourselves. The same is true for cyberattacks." Interestingly, given the sheer volume of screeching about RUSSIA! for the past half-decade/seventy years, Cyber Polygon has featured a slew of institutions housed in Russia and the former USSR alongside Deutsche Bank's Technology Centre (housed in Russia), IBM, and Banco Santander, among others. This is not to suggest that Russia is, in fact, colluding to destroy the West with the complicity of its feckless "elites," although that is in fact a possibility, but rather more so to point out that behind the scenes of this global stage production, distinctions such as "Russian" or "American" are irrelevant to those in power—there is one conglomeration of technophiles at war with humanity at large, although this conglomeration itself does often bifurcate along the lines of whether they are, to borrow from Yuval Noah Harari's book *Homo Deus* (originally published in 2015 in Hebrew in Israel as *The History of Tomorrow*), "techno-humanists" or a part of the "data religion." Harari's *Homo Deus* outlines the data religion or "Dataism" as "say[ing] that the universe consists of data flows, and the value of any phenomenon or entity is determined by its contribution to data processing."[7]

For gay Jewish atheist Harari, the data religion, "argues that humans have completed their cosmic task and should now pass the torch on to entirely new kinds of entities."[8] For Harari:

> *According to Dataism, human experiences are not sacred and* Homo sapiens *isn't the apex of creation or a precursor of some future* Homo deus. *Humans are merely tools for creating the Internet-of-All-Things, which may eventually spread out from planet Earth to cover the whole galaxy and even the whole universe. This*

---

[7] Harari, *Homo Deus*, Chapter 11.
[8] Ibid., Chapter 10.

cosmic data-processing system would be like God. It will be every-where and will control everything, and humans are destined to merge into it.[9]

Though quite possibly phased out of existence by their creation(s), the Dataists view themselves as creators and thus gods. Conversely, continuing with Harari, the techno-humanists also aim to become gods, but:

[A] techno-humanist still sees humans as the apex of creation and clings to many traditional humanist values. Techno-humanism agrees that Homo sapiens *as we know it has run its historical course and will no longer be relevant in the future, but concludes that we should therefore use technology in order to create* Homo deus . . . *with the help of genetic engineering, nanotechnology and brain-computer interfaces.*[10]

These brain-computer interfaces include projects such as Neuralink, co-founded by Elon Musk among others and housed in the same building as another of Musk's ventures in OpenAI, a possible ideological competitor in the data religion space.

According to the publication *Wired*, the genesis of OpenAI began with a meeting between former Stripe employee Greg Brockman and Sephardic Jewish "deep learning" pioneer Yoshua Bengio; initial financial backing came from Musk, the homosexual Peter Thiel, and Jewish artificial intelligence enthusiast Sam Altman, whose other investments include the Soylent drink mixture, which is thankfully not people (yet?), but mostly soy. OpenAI's Chief Scientist is Open University of Israel attendee and Google Brain alum Ilya Sutskever.[11]

In 2019, Microsoft invested $1 billion in OpenAI LP. World Economic Forum partner Microsoft was co-founded by Bill Gates, who is now the top private owner of farmland in the United States with landholdings owned via Cascade Investment, with other investments including the plant-based food company Beyond Meat. For Gates:

---

[9] Ibid., Chapter 11.
[10] Ibid., Chapter 10.
[11] Metz, "Inside OpenAI."

*Cows and other grass-eating species have a digestive system that
emits methane. And methane is a very powerful greenhouse gas.
And so cows alone account for about 6% of global emissions and we
need to change cows. Just cows alone. Of all the categories, the one
that is gone better than I would have expected five years ago is this
work to make artificial meat and so you have people like Impossible
or Beyond Meat both of which I invested in.*[12]

Gates is also a confidant of Anthony Fauci and a major fixture in the effort
to re-make the planet and, quite possibly, humanity. Note that these different strands are all interconnected and the key individuals are all placed
at a very high level of influence. Totally organic, right?

With that in mind, as Harari claims that "Over the past century humankind has managed to do the impossible and rein in famine, plague, and
war,"[13] it only stands to reason that these would-be gods should see fit to
unleash said forces against the people at will, transforming the planet to fit
their vision of the future. For Harari, "Despite all the talk of radical Islam
and Christian fundamentalism, the most interesting place in the world
from a religious perspective is not the Islamic State or the Bible Belt, but
Silicon Valley."[14] Indeed, Harari goes so far as to claim that Dataism might
well have already had its first martyr in the Jewish atheist Aharon Swartz,[15]
found dead in his Brooklyn apartment in 2013 after running into significant
legal trouble on the back of downloading a host of restricted material from
the JSTOR digital archive on the Massachusetts Institute of Technology
(MIT) network.

Whether the vision of the future belongs to the acolytes of Dataism
worshipping at the altar of the Internet-of-All-Things or those of techno-
humanism, for a non-transhumanist infidel it is essentially irrelevant, as
their transformative work will destroy life as we know it, sacrificing the
very essence of what it is to be human if not erasing humanity altogether.
Crucially, Harari writes in *Homo Deus*, "Science is converging on an all-
encompassing dogma, which says that organisms are algorithms and life is
data processing."[16] The dogma is, in fact, a religious revolution as much as
if not more than, say, a Fourth Industrial Revolution, and for Harari, "All

---

[12] Gates, interview.
[13] Harari, *Homo Deus*, Chapter 1.
[14] Ibid., Chapter 10.
[15] Yuval Noah Harari, "Dr. Yuval Noah Harari - Data Processing - Part 1."
[16] Ibid., Chapter 11.

truly important revolutions are practical. . . . Ideas change the world only when they change our behaviour."[17] Change, or transform.

As Ida Auken wrote for the World Economic Forum in 2016, re-published in Forbes as "Welcome to 2030: I Own Nothing, Have No Privacy and Life Has Never Been Better"—sounding a whole lot like Judge Smails from Caddyshack, envisioning a world where "AI and robots took over so much of our work":

> Once in a while I get annoyed about the fact that I have no real privacy. Nowhere I can go and not be registered. I know that, somewhere, everything I do, think and dream of is recorded. I just hope that nobody will use it against me.

This is presented as somehow a good thing, but this Panopticon is anything but idyllic to my mind. Indeed, what Auken—a Danish Parliamentarian, the Former Minister for the Environment in Denmark (2011–2014), and a Young Global Leader for the World Economic Forum—describes as the lifestyle of "those we lost along the way" sounds just fine, actually, and should likely form the bedrock of practical resistance to this project:

> My biggest concern is all the people who do not live in our city. Those we lost on the way. Those who decided that it became too much, all this technology. Those who felt obsolete and useless when robots and AI took over big parts of our jobs. Those who got upset with the political system and turned against it. They live different kind of lives outside of the city. Some have formed little self-supplying communities. Others just stayed in the empty and abandoned houses in small 19th-century villages.

The trouble is these zealots are not content to allow unmodified humanity to exist unmolested. As Yuval Noah Harari writes, "Dataism is also missionary. Its second commandment is to link everything to the system, including heretics who don't want to be plugged in. And 'everything' means more than just humans. It means every thing."[18] In Auken's description, we see a glimpse of a future of bifurcated humanity, echoing Harari, where a

---

[17] Ibid.
[18] Ibid.

new "superhuman caste" ruthlessly exploits "regular" people. Going further, I see no reason why these "superhumans," devoid as they are of tolerance for difference of opinions and disgusted as they are by so-called "deplorable" humans at the moment, would allow for the continued existence of an "inferior" class, especially when they have automated everything around them. For Harari:

> *We are developing superior algorithms that utilise unprecedented computing power and giant databases. The Google and Facebook algorithms not only know exactly how you feel, they also know myriad other things about you that you hardly suspect. Consequently you should stop listening to your feelings and start listening to these external algorithms instead. . . . Whereas humanism commanded: 'Listen to your feelings!' Dataism now commands: 'Listen to the algorithms! They know how you feel.'*[19]

This new religion of Dataism may well spell the death of mankind, or, at the very least the demise of its autonomy. There are a number of possibilities where AI decides to rid the planet of humanity altogether—whether it has achieved sentience or not is irrelevant—or humans as they were cease to be, as they take what the transhumanists would regard as a greater form. As Harari continues:

> *If humankind is indeed a single data-processing system, what is its output? Dataists would say that its output will be the creation of a new and even more efficient data-processing system, called the Internet-of-All-Things. Once this mission is accomplished,* Homo sapiens *will vanish.*[20]

Even should these scenarios not come to fruition, there are still the present issues of the dumbing-down and reduction of human agency via technology as well as social engineering projects, constant surveillance, and persecution of dissidents and disfavored groups, all while not just the gray matter of humanity, but its very genetic code, is subject to constant hacks and forced medical interventions/experiments in the form of COVID-19 mRNA "vaccines." Vaccine in this context is placed in quotation marks

---

[19] Ibid.
[20] Ibid.

because a great many of the new "vaccines" hitting the market are not being conceived of as vaccines in the traditional sense; the Centers for Disease Control and Prevention (CDC) altered its definition of vaccination after the development of the COVID-19 vaccines—the mRNA ones in particular—ostensibly to avoid misinterpretation. Of particular issue was the idea that a vaccine would generate immunity; now, apparently, it is increasing protection. But the COVID "vaccines" don't even do that. According to the *New England Journal of Medicine*, natural immunity provides greater protection from COVID infection than multiple vaccinations. So why the insistence on everyone needing to get these shots, especially the mRNA versions from companies like Moderna? Is it simply to generate more data? We'll circle back to these questions later, but in order to establish the connections that will prove so vital in supporting this book's thesis, we need to note here that the development of the Moderna version of this vaccine (as it is officially defined) was conducted with the support of the United States government, implemented under the Operation Warp Speed program and supported by NIAID and the Biomedical Advanced Research and Development Authority (BARDA) of the U.S. Department of Health and Human Services' Office of the Assistant Secretary for Preparedness and Response.

Operation Warp Speed was a program initiated by then-president Donald Trump to speed up the development of COVID vaccines commencing in mid-2020. Its first director was Moncef Slaoui, former head of vaccine development at GlaxoSmithKline (GSK) and Board member of Galvani Bioelectronics, a joint venture between GSK and Alphabet Inc. subsidiary Verily Life Sciences (its CEO is Andrew Conrad, who is married to the Jewish model Haylynn Cohen). Slaoui beat out Elias Zerhouni (Johns Hopkins, Bill and Melinda Gates Foundation senior fellow) and the Jewish Art Levinson (Chairman of Apple Inc. and CEO of Calico, an Alphabet Inc. venture) for the position. He was succeeded by the Jewish David Kessler (Johns Hopkins, University of San Francisco). Prior to his appointment Slaoui had been a member of Moderna's Board of Directors, and retained over $10 million in stock options in the company until public pressure forced him ultimately to divest.

Moderna's CEO is Stéphane Bancel, a Harvard MBA who also attended the University of Minnesota, one of the main incubators of the transgender agenda. The University of Minnesota also houses the Charles Babbage Institute, which per its mission statement, "design[s] and administer[s] research projects in the history of information technology and engage[s] in original research that is disseminated through scholarly publications, conference presentations, and the CBI website." It was founded in 1978 by the Jewish couple Erwin and Adelle Tomash as the International Charles Babbage Society with its office in Palo Alto, California, very close to Stanford University.

Interestingly, in 1965 at Stanford University, Jewish scientists Joshua Lederberg, Edward Feigenbaum, and Carl Djerassi (considered the "father of the birth control pill") devised the computer program DENDRAL (dendritic algorithm) for the elucidation of the molecular structure of unknown organic compounds taken from known groups of such compounds, such as the alkaloids and the steroids, which served as a prototype for expert systems (in artificial intelligence, an expert system is a computer system that emulates the decision-making capability of a human expert) and was one of the first uses of artificial intelligence in biomedical research. In 1973, DENDRAL was hosted by SUMEX-AIM (Stanford University Medical Experimental Computer—Artificial Intelligence in Medicine), a national computer resource for AI applications in biomedicine. Users at universities and hospitals across the country were connected to SUMEX via the US Defense Department's Advanced Research Projects Agency Network (ARPANET); also in 1973, University College London and the Royal Radar Establishment (Norway) were connected to ARPANET.

In 1978, Lederberg was named President of Rockefeller University, in which capacity he served until 1990. He was also a scientific advisor to the US government including the Department of Defense. Feigenbaum established the Knowledge Systems Laboratory at Stanford; among his doctoral students is included the Israeli-American Alon Yitzchack Halevy, a research scientist at Google from 2005–2015 before eventually moving on to Facebook AI where he brings expertise in data integration, which is useful for predictive purposes and modeling behavior. Facebook has a rather rich set of data inputs with the vast array of personal information entered by its nearly three *billion* users, a pretty good sample size of humanity. If you think the use will be or is benign, consider the funding that helped launch Facebook, starting with Peter Thiel's Clarium Capital in the summer of 2004. We will circle back to this later.

Among other projects, Facebook AI is invested in the Deepfake Detection Challenge (DFDC), partnering with the Partnership on AI and Microsoft, as well academics from Cornell Tech, MIT, the University of

Oxford, UC Berkeley, the University of Maryland-College Park, and SUNY-Albany. Guess who's in the Partnership on AI? That would be, among many others: *The New York Times*; Mozilla; McKinsey; Microsoft; the Future of Humanity Institute at the University of Oxford; the MIT Media Lab; the MIT Initiative on the Digital Economy; IBM; GLAAD; Google; Human Rights Watch; Facebook; Chatham House; CBC Radio-Canada; the Carnegie Endowment for International Peace; Article 19; the BBC; Apple; Accenture; Amazon; the American Psychological Association; the United Nations Development Programme (UNDP); UNICEF; the SoftBank Group; the Australian National University's 3A Innovation Institute ("3A is an innovation institute at the Australian National University intent on creating a new applied science to manage the future of cyber-physical systems—autonomous systems super-charged by Big Data, Internet of Things and Artificial Intelligence"); DeepMind (acquired by Google in 2014); and the ACLU, whose official position is that "Far from compromising civil liberties, vaccine mandates actually further civil liberties. They protect the most vulnerable among us, including people with disabilities and fragile immune systems, children too young to be vaccinated and communities of color hit hard by the disease."

It is worth mentioning that the three countries by far the most invested in AI and adjacent and often-overlapping fields, including biotechnology, are the US, China, and Israel. The Israeli connections include such companies as Diagnostic Robotics, which is in demand abroad for the seemingly ubiquitous contact tracing/health monitoring with COVID-19 as the justification, and in the broader surveillance realm as well. Diagnostic Robotics partnered with the state of Rhode Island on its COVID-19 Self Checker AI remote assessment and monitoring platform and is part of the COVID-19 Healthcare Coalition. Their Medical and Scientific Board features connections to Harvard, MIT, and the Boston-area medical community, and their Vice President of Business Development went to Columbia, is a management consultant with McKinsey, and is a Senior Director with the Clinton Health Access Initiative. There are also Israeli Air Force connections.

These connections are extremely important. I must pause here to both apologize to the reader and explain the purpose of such detail and density. It is not my intent to overwhelm but rather to illustrate that the goal of the "elites" is in no small part to do just the former. Further, they operate using byzantine networks and velocity of data, and model interactions in the human realm increasingly close to that of the machine realm. We are dealing with the onset of advanced intelligences here that are very likely crafting specific scenarios beyond human capacity—but informed by human capacity—in order to further an agenda that may well indeed be beyond human capacity.

I will provide a few more illustrative examples here so that the reader may understand more fully what I am talking about. As with World Economic Forum Board of Trustees member Marc Benioff, Martine Rothblatt—an avowed transhumanist—sits at the nexus of the various strands of this agenda. The Jewish Rothblatt, like the Jewish Benioff, is a member of the Scientific Advisory Board of the Alcor Life Extension Foundation mentioned in the introduction, a non-profit focused on cryonics and helmed for almost a decade by Natasha Vita-More's husband, Max More, who remains an ambassador and president emeritus.

Max More also co-founded the Extropy Institute, which is now-shuttered; according to its website, the Extropy Institute was a "networking ideas exchange devoted to developing strategies for the future. Extropy is a symbol for continued progress and reflects the extent of a living or organizational systems intelligence, functional order, vitality, and capacity and drive for improvement. Extropy is an essential element of transhumanism." According to Max More, the "Extropy Institute is building a culture favoring physical and intellectual augmentation, life extension, and a free and responsible society (here, in cyberspace, or off-Earth)." This includes, from *Extropy: The Journal of Transhumanist Thought*: "Life extension, immortalism, and biostasis; Smart drugs and other intelligence-intensifying technologies; Machine intelligence, personality uploading, and artificial life; Nanocomputers and molecular nanotechnology."[21]

For More in 1993's *The Extropian Principles 2.5*:

> *BOUNDLESS EXPANSION: Seeking more intelligence, wisdom, and effectiveness, an unlimited lifespan, and the removal of political, cultural, biological, and psychological limits to self-actualization and self-realization. Perpetually overcoming constraints on our progress and possibilities. Expanding into the universe and advancing without end.*

---

[21] More, "Extropianism."

SELF-TRANSFORMATION: Affirming continual psychological, intellectual, and physical self-improvement, through reason and critical thinking, personal responsibility, and experimentation. Seeking biological and neurological augmentation.

INTELLIGENT TECHNOLOGY: Applying science and technology creatively to transcend "natural" limits imposed by our biological heritage, culture, and environment.

Extropianism is a transhumanist philosophy: Like humanism, it values reason and humanity and sees no grounds for belief in unknowable, supernatural forces externally controlling our destiny, but transhumanism goes further in urging us to push beyond the merely human stage of evolution. As physicist Freeman Dyson has said: "Humanity looks to me like a magnificent beginning but not the final word."[22]

The Extropy Institute was affiliated with UNICEF-Africa and worked with Friends of the United Nations. Max More was the chair of the board of directors while Natasha Vita-More was the president. The Jewish Marvin Minsky, a Jeffrey Epstein associate and recipient of Epstein funding for numerous projects as well as the co-founder of MIT's AI laboratory, was on the Institute's Council of Advisors, as was the Jewish Ray Kurzweil, author of *The Singularity is Near: When Humans Transcend Biology*. Kurzweil's correspondence with Marvin Minsky as a teenager convinced him to study at MIT; he is employed by Google, which is an integral part of this agenda.

Kurzweil, who in a 2009 interview with *Rolling Stone* admitted that he'd like to exhume his father and clone his DNA, has also worked with the Army Science Board and NASA in the past. According to an interview with *Wired* from 2002 called "Ray Kurzweil's Plan: Never Die":

Just in case he does happen to die, he'll have his body cryogenically frozen and preserved by Alcor, the company that the late baseball Hall of Famer Ted Williams now calls home, to be thawed when the technology to reanimate him has been developed. . . . He plans to outwit the medical establishment on a grander scale by achieving

---

[22] Ibid.

eternal life. . . . I don't think we have to die. And the technology and the means of making that a reality is close at hand.

Marvin Minsky and the transgender transhumanist Martine Rothblatt are now on the Scientific Advisory Board of Alcor. Further strengthening the ties between transgenderism (and the inescapable connection to deviant sexuality) and transhumanism, from the same interview, the interviewer asks, "How does Ramona (Kurzweil's 25-year-old female rock star alter-ego) feel about extreme life extension?" Kurzweil responds:

A virtual person doesn't have to worry about life extension. When she was first created, she was 25 and that was two years ago and she's still 25. In the virtual world they've already mastered remaining at an optimal age. But I do feel that we have other people inside of us. I'm one of the few people who has had the experience of looking in the mirror and seeing a completely different manifestation of themselves. That's what the experience is like. It's like you're looking in the mirror and instead of seeing what I generally see in the mirror I saw this 25-year-old woman. And I could kind of get into being her. . . . This experience will be quite ubiquitous I'd say in 10 years from now, until we can go inside the nervous system and actually create virtual reality from within. That's more of a late 2020s scenario. . . . It's a way of exploring different types of relationships, heterosexual couples could both change their genders, which would be very cool.

Peter Thiel (whose company Palantir is integral to the COVID-19 "vaccine" allocation aspect of Operation Warp Speed, among many other aspects of the globalist-transhumanist agenda) shares a similar obsession with immortality not just with Kurzweil and company but also with a great many of the "elites" behind the Great Reset and the other spokes of the globalist agenda. Thiel, co-founder of PayPal and Board member of Facebook, has written that he "stands against . . . the inevitability of the death of every individual," and as part of his regimen to prolong life indefinitely, he allegedly takes human growth hormone and, according to a 2016 article:

Given Thiel's obsession with warding off death, it comes as no surprise that the Silicon Valley billionaire is interested in at least one radical way of doing it: injecting himself with a young person's blood. . . . Jeff Bercovici of Inc. *magazine published [an] interview with Thiel, in which the venture-capitalist explains that he's interested in parabiosis, which includes the practice of getting transfusions of blood from a younger person. . . . Bercovici notes that Silicon Valley is abound with rumors of wealthy tech elites experimenting with parabiosis, and Gawker has reported that it received a tip in June claiming that Thiel "spends $40,000 per quarter to get an infusion of blood from an 18-year-old based on research conducted at Stanford on extending the lives of mice. . . . He's signed up with cryogenics company Alcor to be deep-frozen when (or if, a more optimistic death-cheating evangelist would say) he dies. There are three ways you can approach death, Thiel has said. "You can accept it, you can deny it, or you can fight it. I think our society is dominated by people who are into denial or acceptance, and I prefer to fight it."*[23]

Thiel has invested with Aubrey de Grey, who is also on Alcor's Scientific Advisory Board, as is Ralph Merkle, a former Director of the Foresight Institute.

Natasha Vita-More was a Senior Associate at the Foresight Institute, based in Palo Alto and focused on the development of nanotechnology. Cofounder K. Eric Drexler's doctoral advisor at MIT was Marvin Minsky. While at MIT, Drexler (who plans to be cryonically preserved "in the event of legal death") participated in NASA summer studies on space colonies and has continued to be involved with research into outer-space possibilities and technologies. He is also a Senior Research Fellow at the Future of Humanity Institute, which is housed at the University of Oxford, which hosts Rhodes Scholarship recipients. Anders Sandberg, a former member of the Board of Directors of the Extropy Institute, is also a Senior Research Fellow. Sandberg wishes to literally become an "emotional machine." Nick Bostrom is the Future of Humanity Institute's (FHI) Director. FHI researchers have given policy advice at the World Economic Forum and to the MacArthur Foundation and the World Health Organization, as well as to various governmental entities.

---

[23] Kosoff, "Peter Thiel Wants to Inject."

Bostrom, More, and Drexler all spoke at the inaugural Singularity Summit in 2006 at Stanford University; it was founded by Kurzweil, Thiel, and the Jewish Eliezer Shlomo Yudkowsky through what is now the Machine Intelligence Research Institute, in initial collaboration with Stanford and with funding from Thiel. Interestingly, Yudkowsky (@ESYudkowsky) tweeted the following in January 2018:

> *People who call me arrogant must seriously not know anything about Jewish culture. Every Orthodox Jew grows up hearing stories about all the famous Jews who got into arguments with God, and the most admired figures of all are those who, like Moses, won their arguments. Like I am *way* more deferential towards moderately superhuman AGIs [artificial general intelligences] than a Jew is toward God.*

Other speakers at the Singularity Summit, which no longer takes place, have included the Jewish artificial intelligence researcher Ben Goertzel, the Jewish immunologist and regeneration biologist Ellen Heber-Katz, the Jewish animal cognition scientist Irene Pepperberg (MIT Media Lab, Messaging Extraterrestrial Intelligence), the Jewish blogger and writer Cory Doctorow, the Jewish scientist and author Douglas Hofstadter, Sebastian Thrun (founder of Google X and Google's self-driving car team), the Jewish science journalist Carl Zimmer, the Jewish scientist and researcher Max Tegmark (MIT), the Jewish co-founder of the Center for Applied Rationality Julia Galef, the Jewish psychologist and author Steven Pinker, the Jewish scientist and businessman Stephen Wolfram, and more.

Tegmark and his wife, Meia Chita-Tegmark, are co-founders of the Future of Life Institute along with Jaan Tallinn (a founding engineer of Skype and Kazaa, also of the Future of Humanity Institute and the Machine Intelligence Research Institute), Victoria Krakovna (a research scientist in AI safety at DeepMind; her PhD thesis in statistics and machine learning at Harvard University focused on building interpretable models), and Anthony Aguirre (the Faggin Presidential Professor for the Physics of Information at UC Santa Cruz; creator of the science and technology prediction platform Metaculus.com). Their Scientific Advisory Board includes for some reason Morgan Freeman and Alan Alda, as well as individuals like Bostrom and Stuart Russell, a computer science professor at Berkeley and the Director of the Center for Intelligent Systems, as well as a Fellow and former Executive Council member of the American Association for Artificial Intelligence. Elon Musk is also on the Scientific Advisory Board and is a top donor along with the Jewish Sam Harris and the Jewish Facebook co-founder Dustin Moskovitz's Open Philanthropy Project. Among Musk's many projects is Neuralink, which is focused on developing implantable brain-machine interfaces. Neuralink shares a headquarters with OpenAI, whose CEO Sam Altman is Jewish. Peter Thiel is, in addition to Musk, a major backer of the OpenAI project.

These are the people and this is the ideology animating the Great Reset (which will be explored in more detail in the following chapter) and the dominant strain of globalism we are seeing unfold before our very eyes at this moment, as it moves from "simply" shadow domination, through the financial system and in influence in other corridors of power, to something far darker, which would see too many of the kinds of connections to the work being done with "living vaccine factories" and *hydra vulgaris* at UC Davis, for example—the latter of which in the Hydra 2.0 Genome Project also includes the NIH. As Anna Wiener writes for *The New Republic*:

> *Extropians [individuals like Thiel and Kurzweil] . . . helped set the stage for a sector of the tech industry that has, of late, been flooded with money from philanthropists and venture capitalists alike. Life extension, artificial intelligence, robotics, and other posthuman ambitions are still very much a part of the techno-utopian agenda, in a way that's more mainstream than ever. . . . Google co-founder Larry Page has invested $750 million in Calico, a laboratory for anti-aging technologies.*

Not only that, but as Wiener admits, "At a time of great cynicism about humanity—and the future we're all barreling toward—there is something irresistible about transhumanism. Call it magical thinking." Magical indeed, if the reader will recall the occultic implications discussed in the Introduction. One cannot help but ponder the animating force or forces seeking to expand and subsume that which was fearfully and wonderfully made.

It is not coincidental that Klaus Schwab and the World Economic Forum's Internet of Things (IoT) and its vast network of sensors and the free flow of information will by "necessity" beget the Internet of *All* Things (IoAT), the bringing-online of an all-encompassing network representing the coup de grace of humanity and—very possibly—all living matter. The

IoAT may well, as Harari writes in *Homo Deus*, "pervade the whole galaxy and even the whole universe. This cosmic data-processing system would be like God. It will be everywhere and will control everything, and humans are destined to merge into it."[24] Provided a superintelligence does not eliminate humanity altogether before such a merger occurs. But, in any case, neither scenario is appealing for those who value human life and/or sovereignty.

When humanity is reduced to nothing but sets of code, cut off as it were from the Creator and the responsibility of stewardship, such a philosophical leap becomes quite possible, especially enamored as he is with his own abilities. In the realm of scientism, which is rapidly displacing secular humanism as the prevailing dogma of the people who are actually designing the systems to replace themselves and/or to merge with their creation, the creation of the IoAT has become their religious obsession. For Harari, "In Silicon Valley the Dataist prophets consciously use traditional messianic language. For example, Ray Kurzweil's book of prophecies is called *The Singularity is Near*, echoing John the Baptist's cry: 'the kingdom of heaven is near' (Matthew 3:2)."[25] Bill Gates describes Kurzweil's vision as "optimistic."

One thing the reader may note is the sheer volume of Jewish, atheist, and/or homosexual individuals invested in this vision of the future. There are, to my mind, several reasons for this, ranging from a messianic void as applies to the first two categories (and more specifically the drive to build the Third Temple in Judaism) and to the specifically-Jewish concept of *tikkun olam*, a concept adopted by many Judaized Westerners and others through key areas of Jewish influence that have come to shape perception. Think of the outsized Jewish role in media and psychology—and their intersection—as examples. There are also certain psychological and mental health factors pertaining to Jews and/or homosexuals I discuss in *The Transgender-Industrial Complex*, and Kevin MacDonald's work also delves deeply into the Jewish psychology that seems to almost invariably lead to support for multi-culturalism, radical politics, and the like. Judaism being largely a racial rather than religious reflection explains behavioral patterns in much the same way we can observe Anglo-Saxon culture recreated across multiple continents that retains certain characteristics regardless of geography. That there seems to be a very clear animus of many Jews toward

---

[24] Harari, Homo Deus, Chapter 11.
[25] Ibid., Chapter 7.

specificaily European and European-derived peoples is another observable phenomenon, sometimes going so far as to in essence wear Whiteface to decry Whites as inherently evil and in need of eradication (see: Susan Sontag, Noel Ignatiev, the part-Jewish Tim Wise, et cetera). There are certainly very compelling biblical explanations for where these tensions exist as well. Though a full treatment of what is sometimes called the "Jewish Question" is beyond the purview of this book, it is something that bears consideration, especially as Jews are so pervasive in the ideology of transhumanism, such a driving force in the world today—and a force that imperils our very humanity at that.

Transhumanism is the feverish delusion driving a great many major figures in the One World regime, Jewish and otherwise, who are fully invested in this image of immortality and certainly have no limitations to their own delusions of grandeur.

"Does God exist?" Ray Kurzweil asks. "I would say, 'Not yet.'"

If transhumanism is a religion, then it is the World Economic Forum that is their Church with its seat not in Rome or Constantinople, but the small Swiss town of Davos.

Chapter Two:
The World Economic Forum
and the Great Reset

At this juncture, it is worthwhile to take a brief look at the history of the World Economic Forum that has given itself the authority to call for a global Great Reset—which, again, *is just a conspiracy theory*—and how its existence dovetails with that of the centrally-controlled One Europe bureaucratic state whose people, according to the Jewish Barber Lerner Spectre, "must learn to be multi-cultural." The WEF's first iteration was as the European Management Forum, with the first European Management Symposium held in 1971 and attended by numerous Harvard academics and other individuals such as: IBM President Jacques Maisonrouge; the Jewish Herman Kahn (co-founder of the Hudson Institute, military strategist and systems theorist for the RAND Corporation, a prominent futurist, and considered one of the fathers of scenario planning); and Otto von Habsburg, the last crown prince of the Austro-Hungarian Empire and Vice President (and then President) of the International Paneuropean Union, which published Count Richard von Coudenhove-Kalergi's manifesto *Paneuropa* in 1923.

Kalergi, heavily influenced by his marriage to the Jewish actress Ida Roland and possessing a strange worship of Jews, is most known for what is commonly called the Kalergi Plan, derived from his 1925 book *Practical Idealism*, where "Eurasian-Negroids" would replace "the diversity of peoples" with a "diversity of individuals." An associate of both Winston Churchill and Charles de Gaulle, Kalergi had a massive influence on the shaping of Europe's (mis-)direction in the twentieth and now twenty-first centuries. The European Society Coudenhove-Kalergi awards a prize every two years to major figures who have proven themselves to be committed to Kalergi's vision, including former German Chancellor Angela Merkel, former President of the European Commission Jean-Claude Juncker, and former US President Ronald Reagan. Attendees of Kalergi's Pan-Europa Congress included prominent Jews such as Albert Einstein and the junk psychologist Sigmund Freud, whose presence especially makes sense if we consider the wider context of psychological manipulation and cooption of the social sciences by ideologues and ethno-religious (read: Jewish) interest groups. It makes even more sense when we consider the role Freud's nephew Edward Bernays played in the study and use of propaganda, specifically through mass media and advertising.

Additionally, Kalergi was a major supporter of aspects of the visions of US President Woodrow Wilson and the gay Jewish communist Kurt Hiller. In 1921, he joined a Viennese Masonic lodge, and the year following, with Otto von Habsburg, he founded the International Paneuropean Union.

According to his autobiography, at the beginning of 1924, his friend Baron Louis de Rothschild introduced him to Max Warburg, who offered to finance his movement for the next three years by giving him 60,000 gold marks. Warburg remained sincerely interested in the movement for the remainder of his life and served as an intermediate for Coudenhove-Kalergi with influential Americans such as banker Paul Warburg and financier Bernard Baruch.

Baruch, the Warburgs, and the Rothschilds are of course all Jewish, and once again we see the role of high finance as an inherently destructive force and obstacle to not just the self-preservation of distinct ethnic groups, but that of humanity itself, as we enter the post-COVID world. Again recalling Barbara Lerner Spectre, there is a documentable propensity of Jewish interest groups to agitate for multi-culturalism and open borders, especially in Western nations although not limited to them; Kevin MacDonald's *The Culture of Critique* offers an excellent starting point on both this phenomenon and that of the aforementioned infiltration of what we now know as critical theory by its acolytes in the social sciences. My work also touches on both aspects and how this is a vital consideration in order to understand the way the world around us has been consciously re-shaped for particular purposes and outcomes. What we will see in the World Economic Forum is that it has proven to be a central meeting point of various interests whose vision has increasingly coalesced around the idea that technology is a necessary vehicle for not just social control and managing outcomes, but actively re-shaping the world around a particular vision that is, to paraphrase Yuval Noah Harari, the all-encompassing dogma of science/scientism. It is begetting a new world of digital feudalism, which we will explore in more depth later.

Schwab's second Forum meeting in Davos featured NASA rocket scientist Wernher von Braun and "industrial democracy" thinker and activist Charles Levinson, who joined DuPont in 1978. Levinson's inclusion is especially notable for it marks the beginning of what we might think of as "corporate activism," although Bernays's work with Lucky Strike Cigarettes could potentially serve as a much earlier starting point. Also in attendance was Pierre Werner, President of Luxembourg, who presented the so-called Werner Plan that laid the foundation for the European Monetary Union and the single currency.

The third European Management Symposium in 1973 featured a speech by Italian industrialist Aurelio Peccei summarizing *The Limits to Growth*, a book echoing the concerns of Thomas Malthus and Peccei's contemporaries, such as Paul Ehrlich, that had been commissioned by the Club of Rome, which Peccei co-founded and served as its first president. The Club was founded at David Rockefeller's estate in Bellagio, Italy, in 1968. This is the same David Rockefeller who founded the Trilateral Commission with Zbigniew Brzezinski (Board member of the Council on Foreign Relations from 1972–1977) in 1973; Rockefeller was also Chairman of the Board of the Council on Foreign Relations from 1970–1985. We will explore the role of the over-population-*cum*-climate change ideology more fully later, but it, along with these major NGOs like the Ford and Rockefeller Foundations who have extensively funded it, is yet another key piece of the puzzle.

Along with the Ford Foundation, the Rockefeller Foundation began pumping significant funding into the Council in the late 1930s; additionally, Paul Warburg was a member of the Board from its establishment until 1932. The Warburgs and other major Jewish Wall Street financiers—as well as other major Jewish bankers such as Olof Aschberg—were the primary bankrollers of the Bolsheviks in Russia, who would go on to take control of the country and numerous others in the USSR and behind the Iron Curtain. Other former Council on Foreign Relations Board members from the past include: George H.W. Bush, Henry Kissinger, Walter Lippmann, Paul Volcker, Allen Dulles, Alan Greenspan, Cyrus Vance, Richard B. "Dick"

Cheney, William S. Cohen, Richard C. Holbrooke, Donna Shalala, Robert Zoellick, Madeleine Albright, Tom Brokaw, Colin Powell, Penny Pritzker, and George Soros. Some active members include Lorene Powell Jobs, Larry Fink, and Janet Napolitano. Notable Club of Rome members have included Mikhail Gorbachev, Joe Stiglitz, and Pierre Trudeau. These are some of the figures most principally responsible for the shaping of the neo-liberal global world order post-World War II and to the present. Larry Fink, the Jewish CEO of BlackRock, in particular stands out as a major current figure, committed as he is to seeding money to the "woke" causes that are proving so destructive to all but the scant few beneficiaries. If there's a common denominator, it's that we all are getting screwed. BlackRock is also effectively the "Fourth Branch of Government." We'll discuss Fink and BlackRock more later as well.

Returning to the World Economic Forum, or what was still the European Management Forum, 1975 was a banner year as hundreds of representatives of government, international governance, and industry were represented, including Royal Dutch Shell, Unilever, and the United Nations Industrial Development Organization. 1975 was also the first year to have a delegation from a non-European country in Mexico, which was led by José Campillo Sainz, the Minister of Commerce and Industry. In perhaps laying the groundwork for the global business establishment's decision to "cancel" the entire country of Russia following its incursions into the Ukraine in the first part of 2022, the presence of dissident Vladimir Bukovsky at the 1977 meeting drew major media attention through his "appeal to Western business leaders to refrain from supporting financially the Soviet regime." As we've just discussed with Western and predominantly Jewish capital financing the rise of what would become the Soviet Union, there is certainly a bit of a false binary here, though the post-World War II Stalinist purges in the USSR in some ways represented a change in direction and of party leadership. That said, the 1989 Malta Summit between George H.W. Bush and Mikhail Gorbachev—recall Bush as a former Council on Foreign Relations Board member and Gorbachev as a Club of Rome member—signaled the beginning of the "opening up" of the Soviet space to the neo-liberal Establishment and people like George Soros and the Western capitalists who would pillage these countries in earnest in the 1990s as the Soviet empire and its satellite regimes were collapsing. It's starting to feel like two wings of the same rotten bird, isn't it? Thesis-antithesis-synthesis, a controlled dialectic if you will.

Also in 1977, the WEF organized the first Latin America-European Business Co-operation Symposium under the auspices of the Inter-American Development Bank, the World Bank, and the Economic Commission for Latin America (ECLA). Further, as their *A Partner in Shaping History (1971–2020)* official history states:

> To broaden its relationship with the media, the Forum shifted its perspective from regarding the press as mainly working journalists covering its events to considering them to be important stakeholders in global society. In cooperation with EUROPA (at that time the monthly supplement of Italy's La Stampa *newspaper*, Le Monde *of France*, The Times *of London and Germany's* Die Welt*) and the International Chamber of Commerce in Paris, the Forum introduced a special series of meetings and publications.*[26]

In 1979, roughly coinciding with American efforts to finance the rise of what we now recognize as the Chinese model of socio-economic control, the WEF welcomed its first Chinese delegation:

> In the fall of 1978, Klaus Schwab followed with great interest the emergence of Deng Xiaoping as China's paramount leader and the evolution of his "Open Door" policy. Deng had initiated a domestic programme, known as the "Four Modernizations", to reform Chinese industry, agriculture, national defence, and science and technology. He was gradually moving China to let go of many orthodox Communist doctrines and implement a pragmatic socialist market system "with Chinese characteristics."
>
> Schwab invited Deng to the 1979 Davos Symposium. While he did not come, Beijing sent a delegation of eminent Chinese economists, led by Professor Qian Junrui, Director of the Institute for Global Economic Research at the Chinese Academy of Social Sciences. The presence of the Chinese aroused lively interest among participants at the meeting, which was chaired by Edward Heath, the former British prime minister, and opened by the French Prime Minister Raymond Barre. This was the beginning of a long

---

[26] Reyes, *A Partner in Shaping History*, 39.

relationship between the Forum and China, which has included offi-
cial Chinese participation at Davos every year since.[27]

At the 1980 European Management Symposium, former US Secretary of
State Henry Kissinger delivered the opening address. Schwab has been an
associate of the Jewish Kissinger's since his time at Harvard in the mid-
1960s. In his address, Kissinger stated that, "Several times, first at the end
of World War II when Europe lost its traditional pre-eminence, then in the
decades afterwards, there developed new standards of power."[28] This
would be the predominance of soft power and the ultimate triumph of
money untethered to labor or commodities that would power the expansion and primacy of the neo-liberal system. For Kissinger:

> [F]oreign policy is truly global. Until the end of World War II, the
> various continents pursued their policies in isolation from each
> other. . . . There are many problems that affect all of humanity: en-
> vironmental concerns, proliferation of the dangers of nuclear weap-
> ons. There is, again for the first time, a discovery of agricultural in-
> competence in many parts of the world that cannot feed themselves
> any longer, either because they do not have the technology or be-
> cause the population has pressed at the margins of their resources—
> of which the reverse side is the near monopoly position of small
> numbers of countries of scarce raw materials. And there is a dilution
> of confidence in classic economic models, a challenge to the capital-
> ist system, but also a demoralization of the socialist systems which
> nowhere have produced the satisfaction of the human personality.
> All of these changes are global and would make ours a period of tur-
> moil.[29]

Capitalist-socialist, American-Soviet, thesis-antithesis. Seeing how this
works?

As the 1980s wore on, the Forum saw a deep commitment from the
Reagan administration, as well as several other crucial developments, such

---

[27] Ibid., 43.
[28] Quoted in Ibid., 51.
[29] Ibid.

as the intentional linking of "foreign affairs, finance, economy, trade, environment, technology, health or other portfolios."[30] Additionally:

> *The Forum took the initiative to invite the trade ministers of the top 12 trading nations and the head of the General Agreement on Tariffs and Trade (GATT) to join an Informal Gathering on World Trade in Lausanne. On that occasion, the group launched the idea of a new trade round. Later, at the invitation of the Uruguay government, the group met again in Montevideo, where the Uruguay Round of global trade negotiations was officially launched. These talks would eventually lead to the creation in 1995 of the successor to the GATT, the World Trade Organization (WTO). . . .*
>
> *By 1984, the Informal Gathering of World Economic Leaders (IGWEL) had already become a useful place for leaders to launch and test new ideas. Many initiatives that were later officially undertaken by international organizations or governments were in fact "born" in Davos. For example, Mexican President Carlos Salinas de Gortari, who spearheaded and negotiated the North American Free Trade Agreement (NAFTA) with the United States and Canada, once said that the idea of the trade bloc had emerged at an IGWEL. The first steps to organize the UN Conference on Environment and Development, known as "The Earth Summit", that was held in Rio de Janeiro in 1992, were also taken at an IGWEL.[31]*

Some of the major participants at the 1984 IGWEL included: Canadian Prime Minister Pierre Trudeau (presumably Justin's father and another Club of Rome guy); Yuan Baohua, Vice-Chairman of the State Economic Commission and Chairman of CEMA, China; Anthony Solomon, President of the Federal Reserve Bank of New York; Alden W. Clausen, President of the World Bank; Pieter Dankert, President of the European Parliament; Arthur Dunkel, Director-General of the GATT; and Jean Ripert, Director-General for Development and International Economic Cooperation, United Nations.

---

[30] Ibid., 59.
[31] Ibid., 67, 73.

In 1987, the European Management Forum changed its name to the World Economic Forum. For Schwab, "We must finally behave as what we are—a global community."[32] For 1992's Annual Meeting:

> *At a brainstorming lunch three young men who would rise to prominence within the next decade were present: Alexei Kudrin, Deputy Chairman of St Petersburg's Committee for Economic Development and now Minister of Finance of the Russian Federation; Alexei Miller, Head of Department of the city's External Affairs Committee and now Chairman of Gazprom, Russia's largest company; and Vladimir Putin, Deputy Mayor of St Petersburg and Chairman of the External Affairs Committee, who would succeed Boris Yeltsin in 2000 as president of the Russian Federation and then become prime minister in 2008.[33]*

That same year, the WEF launched the Global Leaders for Tomorrow (GLTs), which would eventually morph into the Forum of Young Global Leaders; some of the original nominees included future UK Prime Minister Gordon Brown, future German Chancellor Angela Merkel, future French President Nicholas Sarkozy, and Lawrence "Larry" Summers, then Vice President and Chief Economist of the World Bank.

The Global Leaders for Tomorrow Class of 1993 featured such individuals as Bill Gates, former UK Prime Minister Tony Blair, U2 singer Bono, Richard Branson (Virgin Group), Michael Dell (Dell Computers), Edgar Bronfman (Seagrams fortune, former CEO of Warner Music Group), Hungarian Prime Minister Viktor Orban, cellist Yo-Yo Ma, political commentator and TV host George Stephanopoulos, and South African President Cyril Ramaphosa. The Global Leaders for Tomorrow Class of 1995 featured such individuals as Steve Ballmer (LA Clippers, Microsoft), Jean-Claude Juncker, Paul Krugman (economist), and Jeffrey Sachs (economist, former director of The Earth Institute at Columbia University). Other Global Leaders for Tomorrow alumni include Jeff Bezos (Amazon), Eric Schmidt (Google/Alphabet), Pierre Omidyar (eBay/Omidyar Network), Jack Ma (Alibaba), Fareed Zakaria (CNN/*Washington Post*), Marc Benioff (Salesforce), Van Jones (Center for American Progress/CNN), Aerin Lauder (Estée Lauder), Larry Page (Google), and Lance Armstrong (cyclist).

---

[32] Quoted in Ibid., 91.
[33] Ibid., 130.

Class of 1996 member Boris Jordan was a key figure in attracting Western investment in Russia in the 1990s, and his flagship fund Sputnik
counted George Soros and the Harvard University Endowment among its
shareholders. Jordan is a representative figure in the pillaging of that country in the decade following the collapse of the USSR; showing the moral
bankruptcy and the incestuous nature of how this cabal operates, David
Warsh writes:

> *It was in the mid-1990s that, while under contract to the US Agency
> for International Development to provide advice to the Russian gov-
> ernment, Harvard economist [Andrei] Shleifer, his wife, his deputy
> and the deputy's girlfriend went into business in Russia for them-
> selves. The once and future Harvard economist [Larry] Summers,
> Shleifer's old friend and mentor, was overseeing US economic policy
> towards Russia all the while, eventually as Treasury Secretary. . . .*
>
> *[Summers] returned to Washington in 1990 as chief economist
> for the World Bank. . . . In 1991, he took Shleifer along on a Bank
> mission to advise the government of Lithuania. He also enthusiasti-
> cally backed Harvard's offer of a professorship, which Shleifer
> took. . . .*
>
> *In October 1992, President George H. W. Bush signed the Open-
> Market Support Act, authorizing up to $350 million in aid to Russia,
> to be managed by the Agency for International Development. A few
> weeks later, he was defeated by Bill Clinton, and Clinton's advisers,
> Robert Rubin and Larry Summers among them, took the conn. In
> December, Harvard was awarded a USAID contract to provide un-
> biased advice to the Russian government on how to convert its heav-
> ily planned economy to one governed by market principles. . . .*
>
> *It was in 1992 that Hans-Joerg Rudloff, president of Credit
> Suisse First Boston, hired Jordan and sent him to Moscow — the
> same year that Shleifer arrived in town for USAID. . . . He paired Jor-
> dan with Steven Jennings, a veteran of the privatization auctions
> that had taken place in New Zealand during the 1980s. Their instruc-
> tions: find ways of making money in the Great Sell-Off of Russian
> assets. . . .*
>
> *About Shleifer's innermost ambitions, we'll never know, since
> his standing as Washington's privateizer-in-chief [sic] in Moscow
> collapsed not long after Yeltsin's second-term began, before the*

scandals of the loans-for-shares program, before Russia's real estate property laws could be reformed.[34]

What is also illustrative here is the ethno-religious common denominator and tendency to in-group favoritism and collaboration at the expense of the out-group—Schleifer and Summers are Jewish, as are Rubin and Soros. This behavior played out in Russia much the same as the predominantly Jewish bankers financed the rise of the Jewish-dominated leadership of the Bolsheviks. While perhaps uncomfortable to acknowledge, it is an observable phenomenon that often manifests itself with tragic consequences. We can also see the intersection of what are considered Jewish interests—or at least Jewish-informed values such as the *tikkun olam*—with those of Gentiles with their own considerations, where the motivations are not also explained by greed—certainly a major motivator and factor to consider.

Another 1996 "graduate" includes Soros functionary Adair Turner, part of the Institute for New Economic Thinking, co-founded by Soros. Turner is the former head regulator of the City of London from 2008–2013 who first introduced legislation for a Green New Deal into the UK parliament in 2009. New Economic Thinking, per their website and echoing the explicit linkage of causes into a single platform indicative of this agenda, must "incorporate analyses of climate change [and] population growth," as well as include "diversity of race, gender, class, and other forms of identity." The Jewish Jeffrey Sachs of the Class of 1995 was also actively involved in the privatization efforts of the Eastern Bloc in the 1990s like Soros and company and is on the Advisory Board of the Institute for New Economic Thinking alongside another Jewish Harvard economist Kenneth Rogoff, who earlier in his career was an economist at the International Monetary Fund and also at the Board of Governors of the Federal Reserve System.

Returning to Schwab and showing his more "conventional" globalist bona fides, he is also a former Steering Committee member for the Bilderberg Group alongside individuals such as Henry Kissinger, Larry Summers, and Jeffrey Epstein associate George J. Mitchell. Epstein's extensive ties to institutions such as MIT and Summers' former employer Harvard (in addition to the "special connection" Summers and Epstein shared) are well-documented, as was his central position as a facilitator for the vital connections that form so much of the transhumanist infrastructure.

---

[34] Warsh, "In Which, at Last."

Schwab is a dedicated transhumanist and believes in the transformative power of technology. His works and public appearances praise the integration of machines into man, and this is reflected in the policies and the agenda advanced by the World Economic Forum. Keep in mind this is not some fringe organization; it counts most of the world's largest businesses and other entities as partners, including the Gates Foundation, the Bank of China, Amazon, SWIFT, State Street, Saudi Aramco, Palantir, Pfizer, PayPal, the Open Society Foundations, Ontario Teachers' Pension Plan, Condé Nast, BlackRock, Bloomberg, Coca-Cola, Visa, the New York Stock Exchange, Microsoft, Moderna, Johnson & Johnson, and Google.

In addition to the World Economic Forum, Klaus Schwab also founded the Schwab Foundation for Social Entrepreneurship, a sister organization of the WEF, along with his wife Hilde. Its awardees have included people like Rob Acker of Salesforce, Helmy Abouleish ("driving a number of initiatives that address major challenges like climate change and food security"), Simon Bakker (Kennemer Foods International), Julie Battilana (Harvard Kennedy School of Government), Eli Beer (United Hatzalah of Israel), Ann Branch (the European Commission), Salah Goss (Mastercard), Jamie McAuliffe (Aspen Institute), Cynthia McCaffrey (UNICEF China), Christian Seelos (Stanford University), and Jonathan Wong (UNESCAP).

Schwab's work sits at the nexus of much of the transhumanist-globalist hivemind activity and its future direction, and it is worth looking deeply at Schwab, the World Economic Forum, and the tentacle-like connections that span the globe with the aim of totally enveloping it. From 1993–1995, Schwab was a member of the UN High-Level Advisory Board on Sustainable Development, and from 1996–1998, he was Vice-Chairman of the UN Committee for Development Planning. He holds honorary professorships with the China Foreign Affairs University and Ben-Gurion University in Israel; in 2004 Schwab was awarded $1 million from the Dan David Prize in Israel as a present laureate for leadership in "changing our world."

Schwab used the Dan David money to launch the WEF's Forum of Young Global Leaders. Other Dan David Prize winners include World Economic Forum Board of Trustees members Yo-Yo Ma and Al Gore, as well as individuals such as MIT professor of artificial intelligence Marvin Minsky and 2012 Future winners for Genome Research J. Craig Venter, Eric Lander (the MIT/Harvard Broad Institute), and David Botstein (taught at MIT, is the Chief Scientific Officer at Google's "anti-aging" startup Calico).

Venter studied mRNA and the human genome while with the National Institutes of Health (mRNA and the NIH are both vital in understanding the COVID-19 vaccination agenda: the NIH for its role in gain of function research and beyond, and mRNA as the primary vector of delivery in two of the three major "vaccines"—I use the term in quotes as they're not technically vaccines despite being marketed as such—on offer in the US) and eventually left for Celera Genomics, which was essentially in competition with the Human Genome Project for the complete mapping of the human genome. In 2005, Venter co-founded a firm dedicated to using modified microorganisms to produce "clean fuels" and biochemicals called Synthetic Genomics. In 2010, a team led by Venter inserted artificial genetic material that was chemically printed, synthesized, and assembled into cells that were then able to become colonies. According to the Wikipedia page for Venter:

> *This [synthetic life] was done by synthesizing a very long DNA molecule containing an entire bacterium genome, and introducing this into another cell, analogous to the accomplishment of Eckard Wimmer's group, who synthesized and ligated an RNA virus genome and "booted" it in cell lysate. The single-celled organism contains four "watermarks" written into its DNA to identify it as synthetic and to help trace its descendants.*

RNA viruses include things like COVID-19; viruses with RNA as their genetic material that also include DNA intermediates in their replication cycle are called retroviruses, of which HIV is the most well-known. Given the over-arching desire among the "elites" to track humanity through mass surveillance, hack humanity through psychology/propaganda (see Edward Bernays for example), and track *and* hack humanity directly through biology—and among the transhumanists more specifically in attempting to defy aging and frankly nature in its entirety—these connections are quite important. We can also see that the architecture and network of neo-liberal globalism have proven fertile ground for the wide dissemination of the techno- and bio-tyranny we see unfolding before us, often using the language of liberalism to cloak its intent. Indeed, it would appear that the left seems more willing to sign on through this particular guise, but this instinct is not limited to the left.

What the reader must understand is that despite the global and often diffuse nature of the expanding World Online network, the ideology/religion of Dataism and its Internet of (All) Things demand central planning akin to Marxist doctrine. Granted the other features of this network are capitalist in nature, but it is unsurprising that the Chinese model is viewed as most desirable for global control, as it combines the best (from the perspective of the "elites") aspects of each system under the cloak of humanism and various other "-isms" such as environmentalism. That the system is not concerned with the externalities it purports to consider should be clear, but trapped in dialectical reasoning as we have been conditioned to be, breaking out of these constraints is often a tall order. Consider the American conservative, a creature who seldom understands that he is, at heart, still a liberal within his post-Jacobin confines. Alas, our Pavlovian overlords provide the stimuli and condition the response.

Of particular significance given some of the individuals and institutions we've looked at thus far, President of the Rockefeller Foundation Rajiv Shah and Peter Thiel are alumni of the WEF's Global Leaders for Tomorrow successor, the Forum of Young Global Leaders. Other notable alums include: the former Prime Minister of Ireland, homosexual son of an Indian immigrant Leo Varadkar; Yoshinobu Nagamine, Senior Manager of Gavi, the Vaccine Alliance; Ibram X Kendi, the Director of the Center for Antiracist Research at Boston University; Facebook/Meta founder and CEO Mark Zuckerberg; John R. Tyson (Executive Vice-President; Strategy and Chief Sustainability Officer, Tyson Foods); Mirjam Staub-Bisang (CEO, BlackRock Asset Management Switzerland AG); Shamina Singh (President, Mastercard Center for Inclusive Growth); Shou Zi Chew (CEO of TikTok and a former Facebook intern); Stav Shaffir (Israeli Green Party); Rachel Schutt (Head of the AI Labs, BlackRock); Kaitlyn Sadtler (Earl Stadtman Tenure-Track Investigator, Chief of Section on Immunoengineering, National Institutes of Health); Kira Radinsky (Founder & Chief Technology Officer, Diagnostic Robotics, Israel); Şafak Pavey (Senior Adviser, UNHCR, the UN Refugee Agency); Mette-Marit, Crown Princess of Norway; Sanna Marin, Prime Minister of Finland; Joe Kennedy III, a former House Representative for Massachusetts from the Kennedy family; musician Wyclef Jean; Mei Mei Hu (co-founder, President, Chief Executive Officer, and Director of biotechnology company Vaxxinity); Tendayi Achiume, Special Rapporteur on Contemporary Forms of Racism, Office of the High Commissioner for Human Rights (OHCHR); Martín Guzmán (Minister of

Economy, Argentina); Sean Fraser (Ministry of Immigration, Refugees and Citizenship, Canada); Marcela Escobari (Assistant Administrator of USAID); Prince Jaime Bernardo of Bourbon-Parma of the Netherlands (Senior Advisor to the UNHCR and Climate Envoy for the Netherlands); Pamela Chan (Global Head and Chief Investment Officer, BlackRock Alternative Solutions); Ailish Campbell (Ambassador of Canada to the European Union); Mamuka Bakhtadze (former Prime Minister of Georgia); Carlos Alvarado Quesada (President of Costa Rica); and Usman Ahmed (Head of Global Public Policy and Research, PayPal); as well as prominent figures from Amazon, Google, the IMF, various neo-liberal academia networking hubs such as Harvard and MIT, assorted multi-nationals and financial institutions, information dissemination (such as Wikipedia founder Jimmy Wales) and media (BBC, CNN, Bloomberg, *The Washington Post*, *The New York Times*), the medical-industrial complex and Big Pharma (such as Pfizer Vice President Vasudha Vats), and assorted functionaries from the permanent bureaucracy and political realm, among many other areas. In short, everywhere near the levers of power. Starting to see why every major institution was in lockstep regarding COVID-19, for example, with the only real deviation being the degree of harshness with which dissenting citizens were treated?

Among the worst offenders would be the government of France, with its so-called "COVID passport" under President Emmanuel Macron, a former Rothschild banker and alumnus of the WEF's Forum of Young Global Leaders, and that of New Zealand under Prime Minister Jacinda Ardern who, it will not surprise you, is also a Forum of Young Global Leaders alumnus. Ardern actually stated that New Zealand will become a two-tiered society between those vaccinated and those unvaccinated against COVID-19. The medical tyranny has not abated simply because certain restrictions have been lifted; rather, it is continuously lurking in the background of the daily distraction to reemerge under yet another variant or some other virus.

To wit, one cannot enter certain countries without proof of COVID-19 vaccination, nor can one escape the intermittent NPR articles talking about "subvariants" or some such thing. They do not, however, explain the sudden and dramatic rise in what are called unexplained deaths. To the latter possibility of a new virus unleashed on the public, US-financed bio-labs in the Ukraine—much like those in China where COVID-19 originated—proved to not be Russian propaganda so much as benign "biological research facilities" as they are described in the Orwellian newspeak uttered by Victoria Nuland testifying before the Senate Foreign Relations Committee in March 2022. Indeed, according to the US Embassy in the Ukraine, "the US Department of Defense's Biological Threat Reduction Program collaborates with partner countries to counter the threat of outbreaks (deliberate, accidental, or natural) of the world's most dangerous infectious diseases," one of which, of course, was the Ukraine. According to the Embassy, "Current executive agents of the Biological Threat Reduction Program in Ukraine are the Ministry of Health, the State Service of Ukraine for Food Safety and Consumer Protection, the National Academy of Agrarian Sciences, and the Ministry of Defense." Okay, so far so benign, sort of—but the backdrop of what happened in Wuhan and the connection of neo-con Nuland thickens the plot; for Glenn Greenwald:

> It was Nuland herself, while working for Hillary Clinton and John Kerry's State Department under President Obama, who was heavily involved in what some call the 2014 revolution and others call the "coup" that resulted in a change of government in Ukraine from a Moscow-friendly regime to one far more favorable to the EU and the West. All of this took place as the Ukrainian energy company Burisma paid $50,000 per month not to the son of a Ukrainian official but to Joe Biden's son, Hunter: a reflection of who wielded real power inside Ukraine.
>
> Nuland not only worked for both the Obama and Biden State Departments to run Ukraine policy (and, in many ways, Ukraine itself), but she also was Vice President Dick Cheney's deputy national security adviser and then President Bush's Ambassador to NATO. She comes from one of America's most prestigious neocon royal families; her husband, Robert Kagan, was a co-founder of the notorious neocon war-mongering group Project for the New American Century, which advocated regime change in Iraq long before 9/11. It was Kagan, along with liberal icon Bill Kristol, who (next to current editor-in-chief of The Atlantic Jeffrey Goldberg), was most responsible for the lie that Saddam was working hand-in-hand with Al Qaeda, a lie that played a key role in convincing Americans to believe that Saddam was personally involved in the planning of 9/11.
>
> That a neocon like Nuland is admired and empowered regardless of the outcome of elections illustrates how unified and in

> *lockstep the establishment wings of both parties are when it comes
> to questions of war, militarism and foreign policy.*[35]

You might note again the heavy Jewish connection here: Kristol, Goldberg, and Kagan are Jewish; Kerry is part-Jewish; Hillary Clinton's daughter and Hunter Biden both married Jews; and the Ukrainian President installed by the coup where democracy came faster than Jeffrey Toobin on a Zoom call—Volodymyr Zelenskyy—is Jewish. Hmmm.

Speaking of the Ukraine, Daria Kaleniuk, Executive Director of the NGO the Anti-Corruption Action Centre in the country, is yet another alumnus of the World Economic Forum's Forum of Young Global Leaders; the Anti-Corruption Action Centre is partnered with organizations such as the US Embassy in the Ukraine, USAID, and George Soros's Open Society Foundations (see my book *The Open Society Playbook* for more context on this relationship both in the macro sense and in the context of the Ukraine), as well as the Netherlands Organization for Scientific Research (interestingly abbreviated "NWO") and the Embassy of Sweden in Kiev.

Two other alums of the WEF's Forum of Young Global Leaders are Jennifer Elisseeff (a professor at Johns Hopkins University who studied in the Harvard-MIT Division of Health Sciences and Technology under the advisement of Robert Langer) and Alaa Murabit of the Bill and Melinda Gates Foundation. Many readers may likely be familiar with the "table-top exercise" Event 201 held in October 2019 just before the global pandemic of COVID-19; the participants in this exercise, conducted by the Johns Hopkins Center for Health Security in partnership with the World Economic Forum and the Bill and Melinda Gates Foundation, "agree[d] that it is only a matter of time before one of these epidemics becomes global—a pandemic with potentially catastrophic consequences. A severe pandemic, which becomes 'Event 201,' would require reliable cooperation among several industries, national governments, and key international institutions"—all of the major actors, in fact, behind selling us the "solutions" that so neatly dovetail with "existential crises" like climate change and "digital pandemics."

As an illustrative figure, Murabit, per her Gates Foundation biography, "oversees the foundation's health advocacy and communications work, in partnership with the Global Health and Global Development divisions. She

---

35 Greenwald, "Victoria Nuland."

is a medical doctor, global security strategist, women's rights advocate, and United Nations High-Level Commissioner on Health Employment and Economic Growth. Alaa is one of 17 Sustainable Development Goal Advocates appointed by the UN Secretary-General and a 2020–2021 Fellow at the Radcliffe Institute for Advanced Study at Harvard University." She studied at neo-liberal hub the London School of Economics and was also an Ashoka Fellow. Ashoka is an NGO that "builds and cultivates" a network of the "world's leading social entrepreneurs [to] pursue system-changing solutions that permanently alter existing patterns of activity," per their website. Ashoka's partnering organizations include the Schwab Foundation for Social Entrepreneurship ("In partnership with the World Economic Forum, the Schwab Foundation for Social Entrepreneurship is a leading global platform that accelerates outstanding models of social innovation"), McKinsey, and Google.

Speaking of Google, CEO of Jigsaw (formerly Google Ideas), the Jewish Jared Cohen, is—you guessed it—a Forum of Young Global Leaders alum; Cohen was an advisor to Condoleezza Rice and Hillary Clinton and has ties to the Council on Foreign Relations. He is considered a pioneer of "eDiplomacy," the kind of soft power that defines the modern neo-liberal regime, involves fomenting unrest in non-compliant nations, and advocates for regime change across the globe. As Julian Assange writes in 2014, and you might note the rather convenient timing coinciding with the so-called Arab Spring and the role social media played in the narrative:

> Cohen had moved to Google from the U.S. State Department in 2010. . . . [He channeled] buzzwords from Silicon Valley into U.S. policy circles. . . . It was Cohen who, while he was still at the Department of State, was said to have emailed Twitter CEO Jack Dorsey to delay scheduled maintenance in order to assist the aborted 2009 uprising in Iran. . . . The people at Stratfor, who liked to think of themselves as a sort of corporate CIA, were acutely conscious of other ventures that they perceived as making inroads into their sector. Google had turned up on their radar. In a series of colorful emails they discussed a pattern of activity conducted by Cohen under the Google Ideas aegis, suggesting what the "do" in "think/do tank" actually means. Cohen's directorate appeared to cross over from public relations and "corporate responsibility" work into active corporate intervention in foreign affairs at a level that is normally

*reserved for states. Jared Cohen could be wryly named Google's "di-
rector of regime change." According to the emails, he was trying to
plant his fingerprints on some of the major historical events in the
contemporary Middle East. . . . Only a few months before he met
with me, Cohen was planning a trip to the edge of Iran in Azerbaijan
to "engage the Iranian communities closer to the border," as part of
a Google Ideas' project on "repressive societies. . . ." State Department cables released as part of Cablegate reveal that Cohen had
been in Afghanistan in 2009. . . . In Lebanon, he quietly worked to
establish an intellectual and clerical rival to Hezbollah, the "Higher
Shia League." And in London he offered Bollywood movie executives funds to insert anti-extremist content into their films, and
promised to connect them to related networks in Hollywood.[36]*

Cohen is also a former Rhodes Scholar. The Rhodes Scholarship was established by imperialist Cecil Rhodes, who was able to consolidate control
over South Africa's diamond mines through funding from Rothschild and
Co; readers will know his virtual monopoly as the company DeBeers.
Rhodes Scholars are often Establishment-approved individuals, such as:
former Australian Prime Minister and banker Malcolm Turnbull (now a
member of the Board of the "cybersecurity start-up" Kasada, which received investment funding from In-Q-Tel, which is essentially the CIA's
venture capital firm); former US President Bill Clinton; TV host Rachel
Maddow; possibly-homosexual New Jersey Senator Cory Booker; and homosexual US Secretary of Transportation "Mayor Pete" Buttigieg, who famously quipped that Americans concerned about spiking fuel costs should
just use the crappy and/or non-existent public transportation options in
this country. Buttigieg is an alumnus of the WEF's Forum of Young Global
Leaders.

Key members of the World Economic Forum's Board of Trustees include Marc Benioff, Christine Lagarde (President of the European Central
Bank), Mark Carney (Bank of Canada, Bank of England, UN Special Envoy
for Climate Actions and Finance), Al Gore (former US Vice President, pop-
ularizer of global warming/climate change), Larry Fink (Chairman and
CEO of BlackRock), L. Rafael Reif (MIT), David M. Rubenstein (The Carlyle
Group), Ngozi Okonjo-Iweala (World Trade Organization), Kristalina

---

[36] Assange, "Assange: Google Is Not What It Seems."

Georgieva (IMF), Orit Gadiesh (Chairman of Bain & Company, Governor of Tel Aviv University, International Advisory Board at the Atlantic Council of US, International Business Leaders Advisory Council to the Mayor of Shanghai), and Fabiola Gianotti (Director-General of CERN).

With the role and history of the World Economic Forum established, we now turn to the virus Schwab and company have identified as the catalyst for the massive transformation they've been positioning themselves to effectuate for decades if not longer, COVID-19.

Chapter Three
The Branch COVIDians

"Science rules." – Bill Nye the Science Guy

Documents obtained by *The Intercept* show unequivocally the connection between not just the National Institute of Allergy and Infectious Diseases and the Wuhan Institute of Virology in China, but that of non-governmental organization (NGO) EcoHealth Alliance, which also "used federal money to fund bat coronavirus research at the Chinese laboratory":

> *The trove of documents includes two previously unpublished grant proposals that were funded by the National Institute of Allergy and Infectious Diseases [NIAID], as well as project updates relating to the EcoHealth Alliance's research. . . . One of the grants, titled "Understanding the Risk of Bat Coronavirus Emergence," outlines an ambitious effort led by EcoHealth Alliance president Peter Daszak to screen thousands of bat samples for novel coronaviruses. . . . The bat coronavirus grant provided the EcoHealth Alliance with a total of $3.1 million, including $599,000 that the Wuhan Institute of Virology used in part to identify and alter bat coronaviruses likely to infect humans.*[37]

---

[37] Lerner, "New Details Emerge."

In other words, COVID-19 was designed in a lab specifically to infect humans. Further, from the *New York Post*:

> *A letter from Lawrence Tabak, the National Institutes of Health's principal deputy director, to Rep. James Comer (R-Ky.) confirms that the NIH funded research at the WIV during 2018-2019 that manipulated a bat coronavirus called WIV1. Researchers at the institute grafted spike proteins from other coronaviruses onto WIV1 to see if the modified virus was capable of binding in a mouse that possessed the ACE2 receptors found in humans — the same receptor to which SARS-CoV-2 binds. The modified virus reproduced more rapidly and made infected humanized mice sicker than the unmodified virus.*
>
> *Starting in 2014, the NIH's National Institute of Allergy and Infectious Diseases, headed by Dr. Anthony Fauci, funded the New York-based research nonprofit EcoHealth Alliance with annual grants through 2020 for "Understanding the Risk of Bat Coronavirus Emergence."[38]*

Readers are likely well-familiar with the NIAID by now, but Daszak and the EcoHealth Alliance are probably less familiar.

Daszak, as per the EcoHealth Alliance website, "is a regular advisor to WHO on pathogen prioritization for R&D" among a number of prestigious positions, and "his work has been the focus of extensive media coverage." In other words, he's a big shot in the area of infectious diseases. Given the police state the globe is fast becoming under the guise of coronavirus prevention, the fact that the World Health Organization (WHO) has been instrumental in all of this and is also connected to the color-revolution-sponsoring USAID, and with the intersection of big tech and biosurveillance tracking and tracing every little thing, none of this is incidental.

Biosurveillance is defined by the Department of Homeland Security as "developing effective surveillance, prevention and operational capabilities for detecting and countering biological threats. S&T [Science and Technology] takes a system-level approach to integrating information into surveillance architectures." For its part, the CDC "supports the principles of the National Biosurveillance Strategy and, especially, its recognition that biosurveillance is important to national security." This strategy, owing its

---

[38] Zinberg, "Letter Confirms."

genesis to the Obama administration, "institutionalizes our efforts to en-sure that we are doing everything possible to identify and understand threats as early as possible. . . . It calls for a coordinated approach that brings together Federal, State, local, and tribal governments; the private sector; nongovernmental organizations; and international partners. It challenges us to take full advantage of the advanced technologies, new vac-cines, the latest science, and social media."

The further institutional connections and staff of the EcoHealth Alli-ance bear this out, which we will see shortly. For the biosurveillance por-tion, we see EcoHealth's Emerging Infectious Disease Repository (EIDR) project funded by the Defense Threat Reduction Agency, and is partially funded by USAID's Emerging Pandemic Threats PREDICT initiative. Fur-ther, Daszak was named by the WHO as the sole US representative on a team sent to investigate the origins of the COVID-19 pandemic—which, the propaganda reminds us, did *not* emerge from a laboratory funded in large part by Daszak's organization.

Among the EcoHealth Alliance's partners and those particularly ger-mane to the topic at hand include Johnson & Johnson (which produced one of the leading vaccines for COVID-19 in conjunction with the Biomedical Advanced Research and Development Authority of the US Department of Health and Human Services), the John Hopkins Bloomberg School of Pub-lic Health, the CDC, the NIH, the New York City Department of Health, and the United Nations' Food and Agriculture Organization (FAO). Johns Hopkins is where COVID-19 infection numbers and the death toll are more often than not sourced by mainstream media; its Center for Health Secu-rity was a partner with the World Economic Forum and the Gates Founda-tion for Event 201, the "high-level pandemic exercise on October 18, 2019, in New York City. The exercise illustrated areas where public/private part-nerships will be necessary during the response to a severe pandemic in or-der to diminish large-scale economic and societal consequences." Note the date and the subsequent response, both in terms of the Great Reset and Operation Warp Speed with these vaccines being pushed into as many arms as possible in the face of a litany of alternatives, not least of which is natural immunity for a disease with an extremely low mortality rate for those without co-morbidities. In short, they create the problem and then provide the ready-made solution. What may help prove illustrative is the list of some of the "players" from Event 201 as well:

- Latoya Abbott, Risk Management & Global Senior Director Occupational Health Services, Marriott International
- Sofia Borges, Senior Vice President, UN Foundation
- Brad Connett, President, U.S. Medical Group, Henry Schein, Inc.
- Christopher Elias, President, Global Development division, Bill & Melinda Gates Foundation
- Tim Evans, Former Senior Director of Health, World Bank Group
- George Gao, Director-General, Chinese Center for Disease Control and Prevention
- Avril Haines, Former Deputy Director, Central Intelligence Agency; Former Deputy National Security Advisor
- Jane Halton, Board member, ANZ Bank; Former Secretary of Finance & Former Secretary of Health, Australia
- Matthew Harrington, Global Chief Operations Officer, Edelman
- Martin Knuchel, Head of Crisis, Emergency and Business Continuity Management, Lufthansa Group Airlines
- Eduardo Martinez, President, The UPS Foundation
- Stephen Redd, Deputy Director for Public Health Service and Implementation Science, US CDC
- Hasti Taghi, Vice President & Executive Advisor, NBCUniversal Media
- Adrian Thomas, Vice President, Global Public Health, Johnson & Johnson
- Lavan Thiru, Chief Representative, Monetary Authority of Singapore

It will not surprise you, then, to learn that Scott Dowell, the Gates Foundation's Deputy Director for Surveillance and Epidemiology, is an advisor for the EcoHealth Alliance. Another advisor is David Heymann, Head of the Centre on Global Health Security at Chatham House, the British equivalent of USAID. Other advisors include the Biosurveillance Coordinator of the CDC and a pair of representatives of the WHO. The Vice Chair of EcoHealth Alliance's Board of Directors is Carlota Vollhardt, who per the EcoHealth Alliance website, "held positions of increasing responsibility at Pfizer Inc. in global talent, organizational development, and knowledge management as part of the R&D, commercial and corporate divisions." Pfizer with BioNTech produces yet another of the leading COVID-19 "vaccines" in the United States, this one of the mRNA variety. NIAID and Moderna co-developed another mRNA vaccine, mRNA-1273, authorized by the FDA and recommended by the CDC.

Pfizer, whose CEO is the Jewish Albert Bourla, reached an agreement in July 2020 with the US Department of Health and Human Services (HHS) and the Department of Defense (DoD) for large-scale production and nationwide delivery of a hundred million doses of a COVID-19 vaccine in the United States. The agreement also allows the government to acquire an additional five hundred million doses. This is the same Pfizer that is alleged to have paid off Nigerian officials in order to accelerate the release of a meningitis drug that ended up killing eleven children. Pfizer had failed to obtain informed consent from the parents, gave fake ethics documents backing the test to the FDA, and, when the FDA opened an investigation into the matter, suddenly called it off shortly thereafter. A former employee alleges that some FDA officials had inside knowledge of what was going on. According to the employee, Dr. Juan Walterspiel, corners were cut because "speed was of the essence and stock options and bonuses [were] at stake."[39]

Pfizer with partner BioNTech and Moderna, whose Chief Medical Officer Tal Zaks is Israeli, were the two lead horses in rushing a COVID-19 vaccine to market as part of Operation Warp Speed. According to the *Forward*:

> *Zaks received his medical degree and doctorate from Ben Gurion University and served in the Israel Defense Forces as a medic. . . .*
>
> *Zaks was drawn to Moderna in 2015 by its mission to build a new class of medicine, infusing RNA with a set of instructions that directs cells in the body to make antibodies that prevent or fight disease. . . .*
>
> *Moderna is part of the Trump administration's Operation Warp Speed, using nearly $1 billion from the U.S. government's Biomedical Advanced Research and Development Authority and working with the National Institute of Allergy and Infectious Diseases, led by Anthony Fauci.*
>
> *In September, as Moderna's vaccine success appeared more certain, Zaks and two other researchers — Alexander Gintsburg, director of the Gamaleya Research Institute of Epidemiology and Microbiology in Moscow, and Shmuel Shapira, Director General of the Israel Institute for Biological Research outside Tel Aviv — were named*

---

39 Edwards, "Pfizer Bribed Nigerian Officials."

No. 2 on the Jerusalem Post's list of 50 Most Influential Jews of 2020.[40]

HEMED BEIT, a precursor to the Israel Institute for Biological Research (IIBR), had its genesis as a biological warfare unit. IIBR's "homegrown" COVID-19 vaccine was passed on to NRx Pharmaceuticals to conduct third-stage clinical trials both in Israel and abroad in Georgia and the Ukraine. NRx, based out of Delaware, was co-founded by Jonathan Javitt (ties to Pfizer and educated at Harvard and Johns Hopkins among other institutions) and Daniel Javitt, who "has devoted the past 30 years to the intersection of psychiatry and brain science." Retired US Army Lieutenant General, former National Security Advisor, and Council on Foreign Relations member H. R. McMaster is on its Board of Directors. McMaster is also on Zoom's Board of Directors, alongside Janet Napolitano and Peter Gassner (former Senior Vice President of Technology with Salesforce) others, and is on the Advisory Board of C3 AI, "a leading enterprise AI software provider for building enterprise-scale AI applications and accelerating digital transformation." Their CEO explicitly stated that artificial intelligence would be crucial to "slowing the spread" of COVID-19. McMaster was also a member of the Board of Directors of the Atlantic Council, America's representative organization in the Atlantic Treaty Association, which is nominally separate from NATO but is ideologically aligned and does in fact meet at NATO headquarters. It is another of these "technically independent" organizations along the lines of In-Q-Tel and the CIA or USAID and the US State Department. Unsurprisingly, you'll see Henry Kissinger's name among those of the Atlantic Council's Board of Directors. NRx Pharmaceuticals' CEO Robert Besthof has Deutsche Bank and Pfizer ties.

The American federal government's Operation Warp Speed project to hasten development of COVID-19 vaccines awarded Moderna a $1.5 billion contract in August 2020 to deliver 100 million vaccine doses, with a government option to buy up to 400 million more. For 2021, Moderna said it expected to be able to make 500 million to 1 billion doses worldwide. The R&D of the Moderna vaccine was aided by nearly $1 billion in federal funding from the Biomedical Advanced Research and Development Authority (BARDA).

---

[40] Janofsky, "Who Is Tal Zaks?"

Moderna claims in its White Paper, "The vaccine mimics natural viral infections in a way that the immune system recognizes. It's delivered to the muscle and immune cells, which process the nucleotide sequence just as they would do during an infection using viral DNA/mRNA inside the body's own cells (but safely)." We now know that it does not mimic a natural response. And is it safe? That's certainly debatable, were a debate or frank discussion be allowed by the media. Why the shroud of secrecy? And why the centrality of these "vaccines" in the Great Reset? Klaus Schwab and Thierry Malleret declare in their 2020 book *COVID-19: The Great Reset* that "recovery" from the pandemic "will not be possible without a vaccine." Why is this the only option?

We can certainly speculate, as World Economic Forum founder Klaus Schwab fantasizes in his book *The Fourth Industrial Revolution* (its foreword was written by the Jewish Marc Benioff of Salesforce and the WEF, a major bankroller of the transgender agenda) about this transhumanist future with a "fusion of technologies across the physical, digital and biological worlds," (p. 7) with devices becoming "an increasing part of our personal ecosystem, listening to us, anticipating our needs, and helping us when required—even if not asked." (p. 15) These personal nano networks range from "a smart pill, developed by Proteus Biomedical and Novartis, [that] has a biodegradable digital device attached to it, which transmits data," (p. 111) to "the first human with fully artificial memory implanted in the brain" (p. 156) and "designer beings." (p. 154) Already in 2015, Chinese researchers were able to genetically modify a human embryo. For Schwab, the increasing velocity of the globalized world is a defining feature of the Fourth Industrial Revolution, a revolution taking place at exponential speed.

You know what else happened at exponential speed? Operation Warp Speed. The concerns over the long-term effects of COVID-19 are warranted, but is there a need to create a global Panopticon for this disease— or any other for that matter? Humanity has always grappled with disease and mortality, and it always will—no amount of transhumanist biotechnological manipulations will ever change that. But that's not going to stop the people who are committed to pushing the limits of what's possible and creating "man-made horrors beyond your comprehension." COVID-19 has proven to be the accelerant for bringing the digital Panopticon online and is but one example of an artificially-created entity used to modify and indeed transform the world around us.

We can see that the Establishment is priming the population for the continued Fourth Industrial Revolution and the AI-driven future. Despite its sheen, this agenda will subjugate and degrade humanity, and make no mistake, it is not just society but humanity itself that will be modified to fit the vision, not the other way around. As Klaus Schwab himself notes in *The Fourth Industrial Revolution* (p. 25):

> *The ability to edit biology can be applied to practically any cell type, enabling the creation of genetically modified plants or animals, as well as modifying the cells of adult organisms including humans. . . . In fact, the science is progressing so fast that the limitations are now less technical than they are legal, regulatory and ethical. The list of potential applications is virtually endless. . . . It is in the biological domain where I see the greatest challenges for the development of both social norms and appropriate regulation. We are confronted with new questions around what it means to be human, what data and information about our bodies and health can or should be shared with others, and what rights and responsibilities we have when it comes to changing the very genetic code of future generations.*

The answer of what can and should be shared for Schwab and his ilk is, of course, everything. The use of surveillance technology as it pertains to COVID-19 is very much a part of the World Economic Forum's agenda, as Head of Corporate Governance and Trust Daniel Dobrygowski calls this "crisis relevant tech." Much as 9/11 ushered in an ever-expanding era of mass surveillance in the United States, COVID-19 is serving a similar purpose (among many other insidious purposes) both in the US and abroad— both engineered events have been major catalysts in dragging the public along the road to the globalists' future utopia by playing on their fears and using propaganda to mold and shape the narrative. As far as "crisis relevant tech" is concerned, Tim Hinchliffe writes:

> *The WEF openly supports the development of so-called "crisis-relevant tech" as evidenced by its backing the development of health passports, which act as digital records of your health status to determine whether or not you are free to travel or even go outside. Earlier this year the WEF announced it was supporting the development*

and launch of CommonPass — a platform whose mission is "to develop and launch a standard global model to enable people to securely document and present their COVID-19 status (either as test results or an eventual vaccination status) to facilitate international travel and border crossing while keeping their health information private." The WEF also lent its support to another health passport initiative called COVIDPass, which was built by one of the WEF's own "Young Global Leaders," Mustapha Mokass, who used to be an advisor at the World Bank. COVIDPass "uses blockchain technology to store encrypted data from individual blood tests, allowing users to prove that they have tested negative for COVID-19." In supporting both CommonPass and COVIDPass, the Davos elite have made it clear they want "crisis-relevant tech" like health passports to be part of the great reset solution.[41]

People are obviously reticent to have themselves tracked and traced, as the WEF readily acknowledged in July 2020: "Non-mandatory contact tracing apps have met with only limited success so far due to privacy concerns." Consequently, larger carrots and sticks have been needed to coerce the population into compliance, such as bribing them with stimulus checks/UBI and/or framing those who do not accept this foreign material being injected into their bodies as public health threats. Despite concepts such as the COVID-19 "health passport" being labeled as conspiracy theories (like the Great Reset itself, as *The New York Times* will remind you, even though there was an issue of *Time* magazine dedicated to it, and the entire World Economic Forum website centers around it, and Schwab has published books on it), Denmark rolled out its coronavirus digital passport in early 2021, available on the Danish digital health portal, sundhed.dk. Estonia began experimenting with a "digital immunity passport" in 2020, and as of February 2021, the UK government was funding at least eight firms to develop a similar platform. We've seen similar passports crop up in France, Lithuania, and elsewhere. Many airlines have a mobile app version as well. And yet, those who express concern over these passports are regarded as "fringe extremists," criminals, misinformation spreaders, and terrorists— all terms being linked in the flood of propaganda regarding any dissident,

---

41 Hinchcliffe, "Skeptical Look."

be it regarding stolen elections or the COVID-19 medicalized tyranny, whatever the script calls for.

And it really does feel like we're living a script these days, doesn't it? Consider that Mr. Great Reset Klaus Schwab, for example, favorably cites the work of "Skynet" firms in his book *The Fourth Industrial Revolution*. In what really feels like life imitating art, the Belgian digital media company Skynet was launched in 1995—the naming was, in fact, a direct reference to the malevolent AI that comes online in the *Terminator* film franchise and tries to annihilate the human race. China has a national surveillance system of hundreds of millions of CCTV cameras and much more, also called Skynet, which is, according to the ruling communist party, in place to keep the public safe—just like the "vaccines" from Pfizer and Moderna (their mRNA research has been subsidized in part by the Pentagon's Defense Advanced Research Projects Agency—DARPA and the Bill and Melinda Gates Foundation) are supposed to keep you safe, or the dozens of tracking applications that have suddenly emerged to do the same! Cheng Jing, a professor at Tsinghua University's Medical Systems Biology Research Center, believes that Skynet should be expanded upon and should integrate pathogen detection, big data, AI, and 5G. For the population's safety, of course!

Similarly, the NSA has a machine learning analysis program called—wait for it—SKYNET, which is designed to "extract information about possible terror suspects"—you know, like those soccer moms at school board meetings who are disgusted with their children being taught to hate themselves through the indoctrination of the noxious critical race theory. SKYNET uses graphs that consist of a set of nodes and edges to visually represent social networks. MIT's Lincoln Lab and Harvard University have worked with the NSA on SKYNET (MIT's Lincoln Lab, which is a Department of Defense-funded research and development center, has also worked with NASA). Interestingly, we also see that there was in May 2016 in the *MIT Technology Review* an article entitled "How to Create a Malevolent Artificial Intelligence."

Also a possibility along the "terrorism" axis: in the midst of the first wave of coronavirus lockdowns in 2020, the Department of Homeland Security's Cybersecurity and Infrastructure Security Agency began deploying extra resources to advising telecommunications companies on steps to increase the security of their 5G towers citing "conspiracy theories" about their connection to the pandemic. With a number of targeted destructions of these towers by individuals in Western Europe, government officials in the US leaked to the press that any attacks by Americans on these towers could be classified as terrorism—with the definition of terrorism constantly expanding to the point where, according to the DHS:

> *Extremists may seek to exploit the emergence of COVID-19 variants by viewing the potential re-establishment of public health restrictions across the United States as a rationale to conduct attacks. . . . Russian, Chinese and Iranian government-linked media outlets have repeatedly amplified conspiracy theories concerning the origins of COVID-19 and effectiveness of vaccines. . . . DHS is also advancing authoritative sources of information to debunk and, when possible, preempt false narratives and intentional disinformation.[42]*

Ironic, as always, as these people are the extremists spreading false narratives. If it comes from an official channel, the truth is almost always the exact opposite. We're always fighting "extremism," because it's a nebulous moving target.

Skynet is *also* a family of military communications satellites operated by Airbus Defence and Space on behalf of the UK's Ministry of Defence to provide strategic communication services to the three branches of the British Armed Forces and to NATO (this may become relevant in the great chessboard of geopolitics along the fracture lines of East and West in the Ukraine). This is not to suggest that all these recurrences of the Skynet name imply some kind of shadowy connection, but rather that it's curious and more than a little creepy the amount of surveillance infrastructure that's been consciously named after a humanity-annihilating network-based conscious group mind and artificial general superintelligence system.

In any case, unaware that systems logic and inertia will soon render them effectively obsolete—just like the rank-and-file of the medical establishment in the COVID era—the rival faction of soccer moms known as "Karens" are still out there, diligently policing mask policies and ruining Thanksgiving because some of their relatives decided to pass on the forty-seventh booster. Maybe those walking biological time bombs should be

---

[42] Department of Homeland Security, "Summary of Terrorism."

chased down and forcibly injected, or else whisked off to a camp like in Australia (or a "quarantine hotel" as in Canada) to keep their biological (and let's face it—ideological) poison separate from the rest of the population. The "elites" unapologetically using what are effectively concentration camps is grotesque. Irony, as we've seen, did *not* die in the nineties.

Your local Karen isn't just a laughingstock and a nuisance, she's a node in a global network looking to standardize and systematize the humanity right out of us.

The role of these Karens as the intelligence arm of the paramilitary outfits in BLM and Antifa is almost exactly analogous to that of the role of informants for the East German Stasi or for the state during Mao's Cultural Revolution. Make no mistake—they are true believers in the state orthodoxy, trusting the science and all that entails. But what, exactly, does the science say? Well, in faint whispers, the vaccinated do transmit the virus and also get infected with it in large numbers, which by definition means they're not vaccines and/or do not work. Well, that is, according to what *used* to be the definition. That's why the CDC, pulling a page straight out of *1984*, just changed the definition of vaccine from "a product that stimulates a person's immune system to produce immunity to a specific disease, protecting the person from that disease" to "a preparation that is used to stimulate the body's immune response against diseases."[43] So it's decidedly *not* about the science; it's about compliance and public displays of affection for the regime. They are the Outer Party. They worship power. These are the exact same people who feel compelled to put "Black Lives Matter" signs on their well-manicured lawns in the hopes they won't be looted like a sick social justice Passover when something triggers the mob into its Two Minutes Hate. We have always been at war with COVID/White supremacy/Russia/Orange Man. That the Orange Man is the one who greenlit Operation Warp Speed seems to have been memory-holed. Thesis, antithesis, synthesis.

Hillary Clinton, writing for *Foreign Affairs* (November/December 2020) in "A National Security Reckoning: How Washington Should Think About Power," admits:

> *[In addition to] the country [being] dangerously unprepared for a range of threats, not just future pandemics but also an escalating*

---

[43] Loe, "Yes, the CDC Changed."

climate crisis and multidimensional challenges from China and Russia . . . the COVID-19 crisis should be a big enough jolt to rouse the country from its sleep, so that it can summon its strength and meet the challenges ahead.

In favorably citing studies from MIT and George Marshall, Clinton includes among these challenges the need to inject even more steroids into the military-industrial complex and to follow the example of Pittsburgh, "once a center of steel production, [which] has become a hub for health care, robotics, and research on autonomous vehicles." For Clinton, "These two agendas . . . should be integrated," and, crucially, "the United States' security also depends on the control of pharmaceuticals, clean energy, 5G networks, and artificial intelligence." Contact tracing takes on a different hue in this light, doesn't it? Interestingly, in that same issue, Jared Cohen co-wrote a piece entitled "Uniting the Techno-Democracies," which, excusing the farce of what we're presented with as a "democracy," looks basically like NATO and/or the EU. The US has simply been the spearhead of this project for some time in taking the lead from the tail-wagging-the-dog of the City of London before it. Now it seems there may well be no more use for America as we knew it with the breaking of the dollar and the medical tyranny for a virus where:

[A] study of thousands of hospitalized coronavirus patients in the New York City area [in 2020] . . . found that nearly all of them had at least one major chronic health condition, and most — 88 percent — had at least two. . . . The ubiquity of serious medical conditions in these patients was striking: Only 6 percent of them had no underlying health conditions.[44]

This is before considering the roles of intubation and remdesivir in jacking up the death rates. Shut it all down, including the supply chains and the gas pipelines, and keep printing money until the dollar is worthless, though, right?

By the way, you know a product works when the makers get blanket immunity from lawsuits (immunity you don't get from the product, amiright?) and the FDA proposes it should be given until 2076 "to review

---

[44] Rabin, "Nearly All Patients."

and release the trove of vaccine-related documents responsive to the [Freedom of Information Act request]. . . . seeking expedited access to the records."[45] All of this is not to say, however, that you should throw caution to the wind, especially if you are older or have co-morbidities; there are also future factors to consider as well that are beyond the purview of this book. Basically, use caution and common sense and understand that what are purporting to be vaccines are at best a shoddily-assembled money-grab and at worst a Trojan Horse for all kinds of nasty. Consider that, as Daniel Horowitz writes:

> *It sure appears that the more we inject people with the mRNA gene therapy, the more the virus circulates and the more they get infected. All the data from the U.K., New Zealand, and our own Walgreens seems to indicate that the more you vax, the more you get infected. . . .*
>
> *In a preprint paper posted [April 19th, 2022], the NIH researchers studied the N (nucleocapsid) antibody levels of those who participated in the Moderna clinical trial vs. the placebo group upon the unblinding of the participants. . . .*
>
> *These are actual participants in the Moderna trial, and their levels were checked roughly seven weeks after being diagnosed with COVID, plus this was a study of the original strain of the virus when supposedly the vaccines were more effective. Yet just 40% of those with prior infection among the vaccinated group had anti-nucleocapsid antibodies, while 93% of the placebo group did. To be clear, this means that not only is the vaccine inferior to natural immunity, but it is so inferior that it might inhibit your acquisition of immunity to the nucleocapsid protein of the virus even if you wind up getting the virus, which you assuredly will because the vaccines don't stop infection.*
>
> *When you hear the proponents of the shots bragging about antibody titers, they are measuring the anti-spike protein (S) antibodies. The shots code your body to produce the most dangerous part of the virus, but on the other hand you don't get the benefit of full immunity because your body is trained to recognize only the spike, not the main shell of the SARS-CoV-2 virus. The implication of this*

---

[45] Greene, "Wait What?"

study would be that the more you vaccinate, the more it erases your natural immunity, so not only do you still get the virus, but you will continue getting it because you can never achieve full immunity, as you might with natural infection without having been jabbed with a gene therapy that primes your body to respond inappropriately. It is an anti-herd immunity shot.[46]

Ryan Cross reported in April 2020 for *Chemical and Engineering News* that, "a virtual meeting in March helmed by the US FDA and the European Medicines Agency concluded that during the pandemic, companies will not have to prove that their vaccines work in animals before beginning human studies." With this already-questionable (at best) step skipped, the ruling class is preparing for the inevitable adverse reactions as well; the UK's Medicines and Healthcare Products Regulatory Agency (MHRA) was "urgently seek[ing] an Artificial Intelligence (AI) software tool to process the expected high volume of COVID-19 vaccine Adverse Drug Reaction (ADRs) and ensure that no details from the ADRs' reaction test are missed." The contracted agency, Genpact, is a global professional services firm that, according to its website, runs "thousands of processes primarily for Global Fortune 500 companies. . . . Combining our expertise in end-to-end operations and our AI-based platform, Genpact Cora, we focus on the details. . . . Whatever it is, we'll be there with you – accelerating digital transformation." Genpact's industries include private equity, media and entertainment, chemical, aerospace and defense, life sciences, and energy.

Genpact's clients have included Bayer, McKesson, and the Israeli company SodaStream, whose former CEO Daniel Birnbaum was investigated for insider trading; Birnbaum is at this writing still on the Board of Directors along with Board Chairman Stanley Stern, also on the Board at Foamix Pharmaceuticals (an Israeli-based pharmaceuticals company) and Ekso Bionics Holdings Inc. ("a company that develops and manufactures powered exoskeleton bionic devices that can be strapped on as wearable robots"). Stern was also head of Oppenheimer's technology investment banking group. Stern and Birnbaum both hold MBAs from Harvard Business School. Joining Stern (who like Michael Bloomberg also spent time with Salomon Brothers) on the Ekso Board is Ted Wang, whose Ekso Bionics website biography reads:

---

[46] Horowitz, "NIH Study Finds."

> *Dr. Wang is the Chief Investment Officer of Puissance Capital Management, a global asset manager founded in 2015 with offices in the U.S. and China. Puissance was the lead investor in Ekso's recently completed rights offering. Prior to founding Puissance, Dr. Wang was a Partner of Goldman Sachs & Co. in New York. . . . Prior to joining Goldman Sachs, he co-founded Xeotron Corp., a company specializing in DNA biochips in Texas.*

At the same intersection where venture capitalists and hedge fund managers rub elbows with biotechnology, for Kelly Servick regarding Moderna:

> *Serial entrepreneur Robert Langer of the Massachusetts Institute of Technology (MIT) and Noubar Afeyan, CEO of the venture capital firm Flagship Pioneering, both in Cambridge, saw the makings of a whole new class of drugs—and the idea of Moderna was born. . . . If you can hack the rules of mRNA, "essentially the entire kingdom of life is available for you to play with," says [Stephen] Hoge, a physician by training who left a position as a health care analyst to become Moderna's president in 2012.[47]*

So we see the true intent of this research: less combatting pandemics and more playing God. Pandemics *do* provide for a lot of opportunity, however. Think about the true implications of what Hoge is saying here: If you can hack the rules of mRNA, *"essentially the entire kingdom of life is available for you to play with."* Literally billions of people took an injection or multiple injections hatched out of this brain trust of sociopaths and megalomaniacs, with the skids greased, as always, by imaginary money of the great shell game of high finance. And now, "Lavish funding has allowed Moderna to set up production facilities that can manufacture more than 1000 new, made-to-order mRNA a month." As the June 2017 White Paper from Moderna entitled "Building the Digital Biotech Company: Why and How Digitization is Mission-Critical for Moderna" (note the use of military language) notes:

> *The inherent software-like, digital nature of mRNA technology presents the opportunity to build a completely novel type of*

---

[47] Servick, "This Mysterious $2 Billion."

*biopharmaceutical company specifically tailored to explore and ex-
ploit the potential of mRNA science. . . . Our mRNA medicines
aren't small molecules, like traditional pharmaceuticals. And they
aren't biologics (recombinant proteins and monoclonal antibodies),
which were the genesis of the biotech industry. Instead, they are sets
of instructions – a software-like code – that we deliver to cells in the
body.*

It is worth noting that this white paper has been largely scrubbed from the
internet; and what code, what instructions, could this code deliver? It is
fair to ask these questions, especially in the hands of these people. If they
regard you as endlessly hackable, what alterations might be made with or
without your consent, and for what purposes? Dan Barouch, Director of
the Center for Virology and Vaccine Research at Beth Israel Deaconess
Medical Center, says, "The COVID crisis is a great opportunity for those
technologies to be pushed." *Pushed.* Indeed. In addition to working on
DNA and mRNA vaccines, Barouch collaborated with Johnson & Johnson
and BARDA to develop their adenoviral vector vaccine.

Moderna has worked with not only DARPA and BARDA, but also with
Merck, who some readers may recognize as the pharmaceutical company
that manipulated data for their arthritis medication Vioxx in order to hide
the fact that it increased patients' risk of heart attack by 400 percent, which
sounds a bit like what's gone on with the COVID "vaccines" and myocardi-
tis. In sixteen of twenty papers reporting on clinical trials of Vioxx, a Merck
employee was initially listed as the lead author of the first draft.

Moderna, as mentioned earlier, has also collaborated with the Gates
Foundation. When one considers what have been identified as HIV inserts
in the COVID-19 virus by Indian researchers[48] and the role of Bill Gates and
the Gates Foundation so far discussed, the following from a Moderna website press release gets a little more eerie:

*In January 2016, we entered a global health project framework agree-
ment with the Bill & Melinda Gates Foundation to advance mRNA-
based development projects for various infectious diseases. The Bill
& Melinda Gates Foundation has committed up to $20.0 million in*

---

[48] See Pradhan, et al., "Uncanny Similarity," which has since been withdrawn, and also
Sharma, "Sars-cov2 Is a Chimera."

*grant funding to support our initial project related to the evaluation
of antibody combinations in a preclinical setting as well as the conduct of a first-in-human Phase 1 clinical trial of a potential mRNA
medicine to help prevent human immunodeficiency virus, or HIV,
infections.*

Is it really preventative research, or something else? There are legitimate
questions about all of these chimeric viruses, starting *at least* with HIV. I
also documented what could well prove to be highly relevant HIV/AIDS
research and other bio-medical connections in my book *The Transgender-
Industrial Complex*, featuring starring roles for none other than Anthony
Fauci, among others. These are vital additional puzzle pieces as we look to
fully map out the effort to radically upend and transform the globe. As we
are seeing with these various linkages, coincidence is rapidly giving way to
conspiracy. Expanding on the HIV-COVID connection, for Vaishali Basu
Sharma:

*A unique feature is the presence of elements of HIV in the virus. Chi-
nese researchers in March 2020 revealed that "viral protein encoded
from open reading frame 8 (ORF8) of SARS-CoV-2, which shares the
least homology with SARS-CoV among all the viral proteins, can directly interact with MHC-I (Major Histocompatibility Complex
Class 1) molecules and significantly down-regulates their surface ex-
pression on various cell types," clearly indicating the presence of im-
muno-depressing features. According to Professor Ruan Jishou who
led the team at Nankai University in Tianjin and discovered this new
property of the SARS-CoV-2, this suggested that 2019-nCoV coronavirus may be significantly different from the SARS coronavirus in
the infection pathway and "has the added potency of using the pack-
ing mechanisms of other viruses such as HIV." The Nankai
Study had also indicated, "The infection mechanism of 2019-nCoV
may be changed to being more similar to those of MHV (Mouse
Hepatitis Virus), HIV, Ebola virus (EBoV) and some avian influenza
viruses, other than those of most other Beta coronavirus (e.g. SARS
coronavirus)."*

Avian influenza, or bird flu, the kind that saw tens of millions of birds
culled in the United States alone as 2022 unfolded, causing prices of poultry

and eggs to skyrocket and straining the food supply even further. Keep this in mind as we progress. Further, in late April 2022, China—in the midst of extreme lockdowns of mega-cities like Shanghai about which officials were remaining very closed-lipped—we saw H3N8 bird flu jump species to humans. In any case, continues Sharma:

Some other reports revealed that patients who died from COVID-19 had suffered cellular damage similar to HIV and that SARS-CoV-2 attacks the immune system's T lymphocytes just as HIV does. T lymphocytes, or T cells, are key for identifying and eliminating pathogens in the body. They work by identifying a cell infected by a pathogen and injecting it with toxic chemicals. A unique structure is that the Spike protein fuses the virus and T cell allowing the virus to enter the T cell, take over its behavior, switch off its normal pathogen-fighting functions, similar to the manner HIV replicates inside T cells. It is no surprise therefore that HIV protease inhibitor Lopinavir-Ritonavir combination has proven to be effective in treating COVID-19 patients, though WHO for unknown reasons has not clarified the matter.

I wonder why.

As not just a biology-disrupter (and its mRNA "treatments" even more so), COVID also proved to be a major society-disrupter. COVID put pretty much everything online and helped facilitate all-time-high screen times, which have stayed high due to habit and the intentionally-addictive nature of many phone applications; COVID also created far more distance between people in a real sense while keeping them online in more ways than ever. The lockdowns reinforced and expanded tendencies of online shopping and "ordering in," estranging people from the acquisition of their food even further. This last trend is going to prove to be extremely relevant, as we shall see. If COVID has proven to be the lynchpin of the "bio" portion of the bio-digital age, then it is artificial intelligence that has proven so for the digital, and it is to artificial intelligence we now turn.

Chapter Four:
Artificial Intelligence

"The breakneck speed of technological advancement and the fever for auto-mation have resulted in these self-contained decision-makers worming their way into all aspects of life; algorithms aren't just the property of social media news feeds anymore, they're also used to predict consumer habits, make in-vestments, and even determine courtroom decisions. China, for example, is in the process of rolling out a system of 'social credit-scoring' in which data collection and analysis techniques will be used to give each citizen a score. . . . Though this system is still highly experimental, it is a testament to the widespread datafication of the modern world and the increased primacy of algorithms and machine-learning in shaping our day-to-day experiences."
– Stuart Montgomery,
"What's in an Algorithm? The Problem of the Black Box"

Algorithms shape our perception to a significant degree by filtering what we are allowed to see through things like social media or in using search engines. In addition to the very real phenomenon of social media causing demoralization through the creation of unrealistic expectations and the unnatural manipulation of dopamine hits, social media also creates ex-treme conformity. There are lots of social pressures to stay on trend, and this extends to having the correct political and moral—which have become interchangeable—positions. These in and of themselves have become trends as moral posturing about The Current Thing, be it vaccines or the

Ukraine, finds its home mostly online and percolates into the real world. This inversion of what most people over thirty might expect is increasingly becoming the norm due to the prevalence of devices in the home and at school as well as a general cultural emphasis on all things technological and "social" (media, that is). What this is doing—and I apologize if it makes me seem like an old man shouting at the clouds—is creating learned helplessness as everything physical and even mental becomes outsourced and anything less than instant gratification becomes a reason for a meltdown; it also makes life performative, which admittedly to some degree it's always been, but there is a distinct absence of interiority with everything being done for external consumption. Eventually you become the product, the tool of your tools if life is lived in this way.

Ultimately, as things are intentionally made worse by those in power through a variety of methods, people will increasingly look to escape reality through the ready-made escape hatch of virtual reality. We have been primed for years to look digitally for escapism, when so much of our issues stem from the warping of reality and the handicapping of human capability through our various devices. Yes, having things to make life easier is fantastic. Being governed by data sets and not being able to function for yourself is another. We are increasingly finding ourselves here, where humanity is bifurcating into those who willingly or unwillingly will become inextricable from machines and those who will remain wholly human. Interventions in the form of mRNA "hacks" masquerading as vaccines is going to make a lot of people unwitting passengers on the transhumanist speed train to oblivion.

DNA vaccines, which "joined the fight against COVID" in 2022 with ZyCoV-D being granted Emergency Use Authorization in India, are the next step past mRNA vaccines. Per the World Health Organization, DNA vaccines are "a radically new approach to vaccination" that "involves the direct introduction into appropriate tissues of a plasmid containing the DNA sequence encoding the antigen(s) against which an immune response is sought." What other instructions might such a direct introduction contain? According to *The Lancet*, ZyCoV-D "might act as a catalyst for DNA-based vaccines against other diseases, such as tuberculosis and HIV-1."[49]

Inovio and its research partner, the Wistar Institute, for example, are major proponents of DNA vaccines; the US Department of Defense

---

[49] Blakney, "DNA vaccines."

provided funding of $11.9 million worth of manufacturing for Inovio's 2020 trials. The Wistar Institute's scientists feature ties to the University of California-San Francisco, Harvard Medical School, Boston Children's Hospital (all of which readers of *The Transgender-Industrial Complex* will understand its full, grisly significance), East China University of Science and Technology, and the WHO. UCSF, in addition to being a central tumor of transgenderism, is also among the ranks of grantees of the NIH for work focusing "on using artificial intelligence (AI), machine learning, and other methods, combined with smartphone apps, wearable devices, and software 'that can identify and trace contacts of infected individuals, keep track of verified COVID-19 test results, and monitor the health status of infected and potentially infected individuals.'"[50] The specter of AI and the potential ramifications loom large. From *Unlimited Hangout*:

> *A company named Cybereason is here to provide us with a short glimpse of our pending fearful futures. . . .*
>
> *Cybereason's CEO and co-founder is an enigmatic former Israeli Intelligence agent Lior Div-Cohen, often simply referred to as Lior Div. Div, an IDF Medal of Honor recipient and former Israeli Unit 8200 member, co-founded Cybereason in 2012 alongside Yossi Naar and Yonatan Striem-Amit, who are also fellow veterans of Israel's military cybersecurity corps. A scholar from the Academic College of Tel-Aviv, Lior Div afterwards worked as a software engineer for Xacct a network service provider followed by the notorious firm Amdocs, which was accused of eavesdropping on American government officials on behalf of Israel. In between Amdocs and Cybereason, Lior Div was the CEO and co-founder of Israeli cybersecurity firm AlfaTech which is described in its national media as "a cybersecurity services company for Israeli government agencies. . . ."*
>
> *Through their partnership with Lockheed Martin, Cybereason now has I.I.-driven cybersecurity software running on some of the U.S. government's most classified networks, including numerous, critical U.S. military systems.*
>
> *Yet, it's not only major weapons developers like Lockheed Martin who have invested in this hi-tech cybersecurity platform. Reuters*

---

[50] Broze, "Joe Biden's Coronavirus."

reported in August 2019 that Japanese firm Softbank has invested previously in the company, along with venture capital firms CRV and Spark Capital. Spark Capital's investment portfolio includes Twitter, Oculus, Wayfair, Coinbase, Plaid, among many other big players. CRV's investments include Dropbox, Patreon, but also A.I. and machine learning-related enterprises such as Standard Cognition and Dyno Therapeutics.

As with Darktrace, Cybereason offers what is described as a next generation antivirus technology which, instead of responding to attacks when detected, will use A.I. and machine learning to see abnormalities to a network's usual processes in real time. . . .

Cybereason also has links to one of the usual suspects, Brigadier Pinchas Buchris. The former Deputy Commander of an elite IDF operations unit and former Commander of the IDF 8200 Cyber Intelligence Unit, he was also Director General of the Israeli Ministry of Defense, CEO of Oil Refineries Ltd and also serves as an AIPAC board member. This highflying Israeli intelligence operative joined the board of Cybereason shortly after his time spent at Carbyne911. Carbyne, an Israeli 911 call platform which saw initial investment from Jeffrey Epstein, Nicole Junkermann, and Peter Thiel, was founded by Ehud Barak and other ex Israeli intelligence giants. . . .

Carbyne911 have been pushing to be involved in the COVID-19 track and trace apps as well as continuing to try and take over the American emergency services communication infrastructure. . . .

All of these technologies must be thought about, not only in relation to just an election day cyber-attack or a terrorist event, but instead think of this in its original and larger context. The Cambridge mathematicians behind the creation of Darktrace weren't originally looking to prevent a cyberattack on election day 2020. These highflying math geniuses were trying to create the singularity, the creation of self-learning A.I.[51]

The reader may recognize the name Amdocs as the Israeli-founded company that as early as 1999 was alleged as having a key role in the records of US government telephone calls ending up in Israeli hands. As Christopher Ketcham wrote in 2008:

---

[51] Vedmore, "Darktrace and Cybereason."

> Since the late 1990s, federal agents have reported systemic commu-
> nications security breaches at the Department of Justice, FBI, DEA,
> the State Department, and the White House. Several of the alleged
> breaches, these agents say, can be traced to two hi-tech communi-
> cations companies, Verint Inc. (formerly Comverse Infosys), and
> Amdocs Ltd., that respectively provide major wiretap and phone bill-
> ing/record-keeping software contracts for the U.S. government. To-
> gether, Verint and Amdocs form part of the backbone of the govern-
> ment's domestic intelligence surveillance technology. Both compa-
> nies are based in Israel – having arisen to prominence from that
> country's cornering of the information technology market – and are
> heavily funded by the Israeli government, with connections to the
> Israeli military and Israeli intelligence (both companies have a long
> history of board memberships dominated by current and former Is-
> raeli military and intelligence officers). Verint is considered the
> world leader in "electronic interception" and hence an ideal private
> sector candidate for wiretap outsourcing. Amdocs is the world's
> largest billing service for telecommunications, with some $2.8 bil-
> lion in revenues in 2007, offices worldwide, and clients that include
> the top 25 phone companies in the United States that together han-
> dle 90 percent of all call traffic among U.S. residents. The compa-
> nies' operations, sources suggest, have been infiltrated by freelance
> spies exploiting encrypted trapdoors in Verint/Amdocs technology
> and gathering data on Americans for transfer to Israeli intelligence
> and other willing customers (particularly organized crime). . . .
>
> "Trojan horse espionage is part of the way of life of companies
> in Israel. It's a culture of spying. . . ."
>
> Amdocs' biggest customers in the U.S. are AT&T and Verizon,
> which have collaborated widely with the Bush Administration's war-
> rantless wiretapping programs.[52]

Amdocs has also gotten into the 5G game and is part of the global arms race to produce "end-to-end digital enabling infrastructure" across the globe from Missouri to Ireland to Liberia.

Clearly privacy is rapidly becoming a thing of the past as the power players seek to "hack" and control humanity (whatever the justification—

---

[52] Ketcham, "An Israeli Trojan Horse."

national security, a global pandemic, climate change), but what's this obsession with 5G? Well, according to Tom Taulli, writing for *Forbes* in May 2020 with "How 5G Will Unleash AI":

> *When it comes to the 5G roll-out, AI will definitely be supercharged.*
>
> *"AI is a huge priority," said John Smee, who is the VP of engineering and head of 5G R&D for Qualcomm. "We are seeing a transformation happening, with AI going from the cloud to being distributed, such as on the edge or IoT devices."*
>
> *In preparation for this, Qualcomm has been embedding AI capabilities on its chips. Note that its AI engine has applications for cameras, battery life, security and gaming—allowing for neural network processing.*
>
> *"5G will cause a proliferation in sensors all around us, and each one of those sensors is a new input available to create better models," said Jake Moskowitz, who is the Head of the Emodo Institute at Ericsson Emodo. "Many of these 5G sensors will directly enable vast data aggregation for remote monitoring and immediate reaction. In some cases, there will be opportunities to use those sensors as AI inputs. In other cases, there will be new AI efforts that require the distribution of new sensors."*

These sensors can help form the bedrock of the new "smart cities" fantasized about by the World Economic Forum, where they suppose a hive-like humanity can be accommodated in the near future.

Returning to the intersection of COVID and artificial intelligence—and also HIV/AIDS—it should surprise precisely no one that the Biden administration's Coronavirus Task Force is, as Derrick Broze puts it, a "Rockefeller, Council on Foreign Relations, Gates Foundation swamp." For Broze:

> *Biden announced that his Coronavirus Task Force would be chaired by former Surgeon General Vivek Murthy, former Food and Drug Administration commissioner David Kessler and Yale University's Dr. Marcella Nunez-Smith. . . .*
>
> *[A]t least six members of the 13-member Task Force have worked directly with Gates or the Gates Foundation, while at least 3 others have tangential connections to Gates. Several members also*

have connections to the Rockefeller Foundation, which is also infamous for shaping international health policy. . . .

[One example is] Dr. Eric Goosby . . . an infectious disease expert and professor of medicine at the University of California, San Francisco, School of Medicine. During the Clinton administration Goosby was the founding director of the largest federally funded HIV/AIDS program. Goosby was also part of a 25-member commission convened by the Rockefeller Foundation and Boston University which focused on "how global decision-makers can better use burgeoning data on the wide range of factors influencing people's health."

In 2012, he participated in a panel with Bill Gates as part of the International AIDS Conference. . . .

The presence of counter-terrorism experts, a Council on Foreign Relations fellow, an In-Q-Tel executive, connections to the Gates Foundation and the Rockefeller Foundation are all signs that Joe Biden's Coronavirus Task Force will carry on the trends started under the Trump administration's Operation Warp Speed.

The Board of Trustees of In-Q-Tel includes individuals such as former CIA Director George Tenet. According to its website:

The CIA and government agencies, once innovation leaders, recognized they were missing out on the cutting-edge, innovative, and impactful technologies coming out of Silicon Valley and beyond. Combining the security savvy of government with the can-do curiosity of Silicon Valley, In-Q-Tel is born. . . . [Eventually] B.Next was founded – and was prescient – in its application of biotechnology to address the national security threat of infectious disease epidemics and pandemics.

B.Next is but one project of In-Q-Tel, but it is highly relevant in its focus to the agenda being discussed.

Also on In-Q-Tel's Board is A. B. Krongard, who helped underwrite Microsoft and AOL as head of Alex. Brown; Krongard and Tenet spearheaded the launch of In-Q-Tel. A complete picture of the interconnections among this web of players is unknown, but, if we can already highlight significant connections, then surely there are many more behind the scenes.

In any case, In-Q-Tel bears scrutiny as essentially the CIA's venture capital arm and these interconnections. For example, Facebook in its nascent stages (summer 2004) received funding from Peter Thiel's Clarium Capital. Major funding followed to the tune of $12.7 million from Thiel and Accel Partners in May 2005 and $27.5 million from Thiel, Accel, and Greylock Partners in April 2006. What do these funding sources have in common? As Jody Chudley writes for *St. Paul's Research*:

> Just for fun, I searched for each of those investors and In-Q-Tel at the same time.
> Here is what I found:
> Peter Thiel — Took In-Q-Tel funding for his startup firm Palantir somewhere around 2004.
> Accel Partners — In 2004, Accel partner James Breyer sat on the board of directors of military defense contractor BBN with In-Q-Tel's CEO Gilman Louie. [In 2018, Louie was appointed to the United States National Security Commission for Artificial Intelligence]
> Greylock Partners — Howard Cox, the head of Greylock, served directly on In-Q-Tel's board of directors.

In 2004, Google acquired Keyhole, which had been contracted by In-Q-Tel and is now known as Google Earth. In 2010, Google and In-Q-Tel made a joint investment in a company called Recorded Future, which provides services related to predictive event planning, cyber security, and other processing and analysis services based on machine learning. In 2019, venture capital and private equity firm Insight Partners, which has made investments in companies like Twitter and Tumblr (a major vehicle for recruitment of minors for transgender groomers), acquired Recorded Future. Noah Shachtman, writing for *Wired*, described Recorded Future as "a company that strips out from web pages the sort of who, what, when, where, why — sort of who's involved . . . where are they going, what kind of events are they going to." "We can assemble actual real-time dossiers on people," co-founder Christopher Ahlberg says.[53]

Yes, there is some superficial plausible deniability here, but let's be real. With CIA funding and people like Krongard, Tenet, and former CIA Deputy Director for Intelligence and President and Vice Chairman of

---

53 Shachtman, "Exclusive: Google, CIA Invest."

Kissinger Associates Jami Miscik (who is also a Board member of the Council on Foreign Relations) on the Board of Trustees, how independent is In-Q-Tel really? Regardless of whether it is or is not actually carrying out direct orders from the CIA, the links with both the agency and other major globalist network hubs—especially in context—are plenty damning and do much to illustrate what's going on here, namely in these instances that technology is not an aid for people or a way to make life easier, but rather a way to track and trace them in real time. Nothing moves without the intermediary, as it were. Further, predictive planning allows for the anticipation of human actions, particularly resistance to this agenda. It is security, sure, but security for the vast bureaucratic apparatus and its shadowy machinations.

Artificial intelligence is in many ways the key to the globalist Panopticon, beyond being a sort of deity in its own right for the transhumanists. So it's interesting that In-Q-Tel President and CEO Chris Darby is also on the National Security Commission for Artificial Intelligence. 2020 investments by In-Q-Tel include Morpheus Space ("disrupting the NewSpace industry by introducing Agile Constellations, a fusion between cutting edge propulsion and AI"), AI.Reverie ("A leading provider of synthetic data to train machine learning algorithms"), and Snorkel AI (based out of Palo Alto). Other major recent investments include all kinds of data storage, sensor network, micro surveillance, and quantum computing start-ups. One of the premier investments on the quantum computing side is D-Wave Systems based out of British Columbia, Canada. Major customers include Google, NASA, the Los Alamos National Lab, Lockheed Martin, and the University of Southern California. We also see investments such as Algorithmic ("Infrastructure for deploying and scaling AI/ML models") and at least eighteen biotechnology start-ups such as Microchip Biotechnologies and Boreal Genomics (DNA fingerprints).

In-Q-Tel made a major investment in a company called Digital Reasoning in 2010. Digital Reasoning signed a contract with the National Ground Intelligence Center of the US Army Intelligence and Security Command in 2004 for the use of its Synthesys software, which has been used in Afghanistan to track combatants. I wonder if it will be used for the same on the new "domestic terrorists" complaining about critical race theory being taught in schools in the United States? Major investors in the company also include BNP Paribas, Barclays, and Goldman Sachs. The Jewish Steven A. Cohen's Point72 Asset Management is one of the major firms that uses the Synthesys software in the private sector, primarily to scan internal e-mails between employees for "unfamiliar patterns" and "unusual behavior."

Indeed, Point72 also retained the services of Peter Thiel's Palantir Technologies in 2014 for "a new tool for compliance and surveillance." Palantir has not only also received financial backing from In-Q-Tel, but its clients past and present include the CIA directly, the DHS, NSA, CDC, FBI, and the Air Force, as well as the UK's NHS for COVID-19-related tracking (ostensibly)—the same UK where the minister responsible for the COVID-19 "vaccine" rollout, Nadhim Zahawi, stated that:

> *Google, Facebook and Twitter should do more to fact-check oppos-ing views of vaccines.*
>
> *Asked by the BBC if there would be an immunity passport, Za-hawi said a person's COVID-19 vaccine status might be included in a phone app that would inform local doctors of a person's status.*
>
> *"But also I think you'd probably find that restaurants and bars and cinemas and other venues, sports venues, will probably also use that system as they've done with the app," Zahawi told the BBC. [This is already being done in Los Angeles.]*
>
> *"The sort of pressure will come both ways: from service provid-ers — who will say 'look, demonstrate to us that you have been vac-cinated' — but also we will make the technology as easy and acces-sible as possible. . . ."*
>
> *Asked if it would become virtually impossible to do anything without the vaccine, Zahawi said: "I think people have to make a de-cision but I think you'll probably find many service providers will want to engage in this in the way they did with the app."*[54]

In other words, even if it isn't mandated *de jure*, it will be *de facto*, with existence within the system made impossible for those who decline to be injected with the "vaccine"—or for anyone who runs afoul of the regime or who has a low social credit score for that matter. Already in early December 2020 companies were publicly considering the idea that employees who refused the vaccine could be terminated; labor and employment attorneys such as Rogge Dunn stated that, "Under the law, an employer can force an employee to get vaccinated, and if they don't, fire them."[55] While there may

---

[54] Reuters Staff, "No COVID-19 Vaccine."
[55] Sigalos, "Yes, your boss can."

be the possibility of temporary exemptions, this will eventually no longer be an option. Indeed, this policy has already been enacted in many jurisdictions. This naturally begs the question why—why are they so eager to get these shots into people's arms?

Now we return to the thickening plot: two more In-Q-Tel investments include Nozomi Networks and Nanosys, a nanotechnology company that designs, develops, and manufactures quantum dot materials. Regarding the former, Deloitte, GE Power, and BT are some of their Global Strategic Alliance partners. Nozomi Networks Labs also launched a "special initiative to help the security community fight COVID-19-related cyber threats." Nozomi Networks CEO Edgard Capdevielle states that, "We're stronger than ever and ready to take OT and IoT security to the next level."[56] IoT is the Internet of Things, a major fixation of Schwab and the World Economic Forum. In short, it is the vast network of physical objects embedded with the requisite technology and software to plug in to the internet and coordinate and exchange data, basically what Elon Musk's Neuralink wants to put in your brain. Essentially, the IoT is any "smart" device/appliance/etc. and will soon be possible to include human beings if the transhumanists have their way. The term Internet of Things owes its origin to Kevin Ashton, co-founder of MIT's Auto-ID Center. According to a Nozomi Networks press release from July 2020:

New customers around the globe [include] key wins at top pharmaceutical manufacturers, transportation companies, electric and water utilities, oil & gas companies and healthcare organizations. . . .

"Nozomi Networks' use of machine learning enables them to provide advanced device identification, behavioral analysis, and anomaly detection capabilities through passive monitoring of IoT and OT networks. This level of visibility is essential for protecting critical infrastructure devices and networks. Their solution is designed to support distributed network architectures and integration with a broad range of security products, making it well suited for deployment into the challenging and diverse operating environments of the U.S. intelligence and defense communities," [says] Brinda Jadeja, Senior Partner, Investments, In-Q-Tel. . . .

---

[56] Nozomi Networks, "Nozomi Networks Announces."

> *We [Nozomi Networks] continue to build our relationship with the Maryland Innovation and Security Institute (MISI). Nozomi Networks is engaged in MISI's Dreamport U.S. Cyber Command mission accelerator, focused on helping over 300,000 Defense Industrial Base contractors meet new certification requirements to ensure better cybersecurity for the DoD supply chain.[57]*

As COVID-19 "necessitated" the need to become more interconnected and digitized, now we are warned of the "unprecedented" and ever-rising cyber threat, especially to the power grid that serves as the lifeline for contemporary society. Cyber Polygon, supported by the World Economic Forum's Centre for Cybersecurity, declared that "In 2020 the central theme for the Cyber Polygon live stream was the prevention of a *'digital pandemic'*: how to prevent a crisis and to reinforce cybersecurity on all levels"[58]—more predictive programming from these would-be masters of humans and cyberkind. Partners for the Centre for Cybersecurity Platform more broadly include elites in the corporate, academic, and NGO world: the Carnegie Endowment for International Peace, EUROPOL, the University of Oxford, Amazon, Bank of America, BlackRock, the Saudi Arabia National Cybersecurity Authority, PayPal, Mastercard, JP Morgan Chase, Microsoft, Huawei, China Southern Power Grid, China Datang, State Grid Corporation of China, Palantir, and the Israel National Cyber Directorate.

Circling back to A. B. Krongard, he may well have been the connection between Erik Prince of Blackwater Security Consulting and the CIA. In 2007 there was controversy over whether Krongard had joined Blackwater as a member of its Advisory Board. His brother Howard was accused of averting probes into contracting fraud in Iraq and a possible conflict of interest regarding investigations into Blackwater. A. B. Krongard was named Executive Director of the CIA in March 2001, having joined the agency in 1998 as a consultant to Director George Tenet. The 9/11 Commission Report mentions a connection to possible insider trading through trades made by Alex. Brown & Sons, where Krongard had risen to become Chief Executive Officer and Chairman of the Board prior to joining the CIA in 1998:

> *A single U.S.-based institutional investor with no conceivable ties to al Qaeda purchased 95 percent of the UAL puts on September 6*

---

57 Ibid.
58 "Cyber Polygon," WEF.

(2001) as part of a strategy that also included buying 115,000 shares of American on September 10. Similarly, much of the seemingly suspicious trading on September 10 was traced to a specific U.S.-based options trading newsletter . . . which recommended these trades.[59]

There is also a theory that the "single U.S.-based institutional investor" might be Mayo Shattuck III, who helped Krongard engineer a merger with Bankers Trust in 1997 and remained after its acquisition by Deutsche Bank in 1999. Shattuck eventually became Chairman of the Board of Deutsche Bank Alex. Brown, before resigning on September 12th, 2001. Shattuck is Vice Chairman *ex officio* of Johns Hopkins Medicine's Board of Trustees.

Why would someone buy shares of American Airlines on September 10th? What happened the very next day involving American Airlines killed thousands of Americans, ushered in a massive erosion of civil liberties, and caused a string of Vietnams-in-the-desert with nations ruined and hundreds of thousands if not millions dead. We're not meant to make anything of it, as the investigation concluded that the trades were "innocuous."

Krongard is also on Apollo Global Management's Board of Directors with wealthy and powerful Jews Leon Black (co-founder, Chairman, and CEO of Apollo) and New England Patriots football franchise owner Robert Kraft. Black, *The New York Times* reported, paid Jeffrey Epstein at least $50 million between 2012 and 2017. Krongard's wife was a senior partner of Apollo Global Management from January 2002 to December 2004. From 1994 to 2000, she served as the Chief Executive Officer of Rothschild Asset Management and as Senior Managing Director for Rothschild North America. Additionally, she served as a director of Rothschild North America, Rothschild Asset Management, Rothschild Asset Management BV, and Rothschild Realty Inc. and as Managing Member of Rothschild Recovery Fund. She served as a director of US Airways Group Inc. from 2003 until its merger with American Airlines.

While Shattuck is Vice Chairman *ex officio* of Johns Hopkins Medicine's Board of Trustees, Krongard is an Emeritus Trustee of Johns Hopkins Medicine, as is Sharon Percy Rockefeller, who like Klaus Schwab, Larry Summers, Henry Kissinger, Edmond de Rothschild, and others is a former Steering Committee member of the Bilderberg Group. The Jewish Jeff Aronson is on the Johns Hopkins Medicine Board of Trustees—is a former

---

[59] 9/11 Commission, *9/11 Commission Report*, 499, footnote 130.

Chair of it—and was Senior Corporate Counsel at LF Rothschild. His Centerbridge Partners has tens of billions of dollars in capital, focusing on private equity, distressed securities, and credit investments. His philanthropy focuses primarily on Jewish causes and organizations, such as Birthright Israel. The Jewish President of Johns Hopkins, which mandated COVID "vaccination" for university attendance, Ronald J. Daniels is on the Board of BridgeBio Pharma, a biotechnology company. BridgeBio co-founder Andrew Lo is based out of MIT, and among his roles is included being a principal investigator at the Computer Science and Artificial Intelligence Laboratory. He also appeared on an episode of NPR's *Freakonomics* in August 2020 alongside Moderna's Tal Zaks and former Obama-nominated FDA Commissioner Peggy Hamburg giving positive publicity to what was then "this first U.S. vaccine candidate." Hamburg, for the record, is married to Peter Fitzhugh Brown, an artificial intelligence expert and CEO of the Renaissance Technologies hedge fund.

On October 29th, 2019, Hamburg was part of a panel including Anthony Fauci speaking at the Milken Institute's Future of Health Summit at an event entitled "Making Influenza History: The Quest for a Universal Vaccine." The Milken Institute was founded by the Jewish Michael Milken, who was indicted by a federal grand jury in March 1989 on 98 counts of racketeering and fraud in an insider trading investigation. Then-BARDA Director Rick Bright stated that, "The sense of urgency needs to be there" responding to moderator Michael Specter, staff writer for *The New Yorker* and an Adjunct Professor of Bioengineering at Stanford, who would go on to ask rhetorically, "Why don't we blow the system up?" before continuing, "Obviously we can't just turn off the spigot on the system we have and say everyone in the world should get this flu vaccine we haven't given to anyone yet, but there must be some way. . . ." speaking of course about "harnessing new vaccine technologies" which, naturally, everyone should take.[60] For Bright—and this is directly from the horse's mouth eleven days after Event 201 with Johns Hopkins, the World Economic Forum, and the Gates Foundation *in 2019*—talking about printing mRNA vaccines from a 3-D printer:

> *If we can move into more synthetic . . . messenger RNA base those sequences can be graphically shared around the world. . . . We*

---

[60] C-Span, "Universal Flu Vaccination."

haven't demonstrated the true effectiveness and ability of the vaccine but it's not too crazy to think that an outbreak of a novel avian virus could occur in China somewhere we could get the RNA sequence from that and beam it [out]. . . . The technology is there to be adapted and assembled and put into the futuristic view of rapid response to an emerging threat.[61]

For Hamburg, "You talked about PR before, we haven't done a good job of that and I think that will help . . . generate the resources." The Gates Foundation was of course favorably mentioned, after which Bright noted "It's just not sexy anymore"—talking about influenza vaccines—"when I was in grad school everyone was working on HIV vaccines. . . . I was in the laboratory . . . working on DNA vaccines for HIV. . . . But in order to make [flu vaccines] sexy, I like the concept disrupting this field."[62] Now granted they are talking about influenza, not coronavirus, however we can see the groundwork being laid for seizing on some massively disruptive event like the Spanish Flu in 1918, for example, and using it as a means in this instance to introduce experimental gene therapies under the guise of vaccination. Influenza in this instance should be treated as a placeholder for what CEPI—the Coalition for Epidemic Preparedness Innovations, launched at the World Economic Forum's Annual Meeting in Davos in 2017—calls "Disease X."

Johns Hopkins Medicine Deputy Director Anito Cicero's expertise areas according to Johns Hopkins Medicine's website include biosecurity, bio surveillance, and international disease surveillance, and her professional profile informs that she "has also launched a number of initiatives to improve mutual understanding and collaboration with countries including the People's Republic of China," and that Cicero's work as an attorney "required constructive engagement with members of Congress; the World Health Organization; the European Commission; the US Food and Drug Administration; the US Departments of State, Defense, and Health and Human Services; and the Environmental Protection Agency."

The CEO of Johns Hopkins Medicine is Bayside, Queens native Paul Rothman; he attended MIT, accepted a postdoctoral fellowship at Columbia University prior to joining its medical school faculty, and is on the

---

[61] Ibid.
[62] Ibid.

Board of Merck. In a July 2020 interview with The Media Line, Rothman favorably stated that big data sets assisted by artificial intelligence technologies could help doctors personalize treatments for coronavirus, with an emphasis on the predictive aspects. That same month, the Johns Hopkins Center for Health Security published a report entitled *Resetting Our Response: Changes Needed in the US Approach to COVID-19*: "Unlike many countries in the world, the United States is not currently on course to get control of this epidemic. It's time to reset." Reset you say? That sounds awfully familiar.

The Rockefeller Foundation, in addition to its role in consolidating control over the global food supply and its other extensive activities contributing to the creation of the One World government, has been gaming these scenarios out ahead of time; they have been poised to leap for some time. In their May 2010 report with Global Business Network entitled *Scenarios for the Future of Technology and International Development*, we see favorable citations of the work of the RAND Corporation, the UN Millennium Project, and the World Bank. For then-President the Jewish Judith Rodin (honorary degree from Johns Hopkins, Council on Foreign Relations, "a sought-after speaker for influential global forums, including the World Economic Forum," member of the audit committee for BlackRock's Closed End Fund,), writing in a sort of preface in the document,

> One important—and novel—component of our strategy toolkit is scenario planning, a process of creating narratives about the future based on factors likely to affect a particular set of challenges and opportunities. We believe that scenario planning has great potential for use in philanthropy to identify unique interventions, simulate and rehearse important decisions that could have profound implications, and highlight previously undiscovered areas of connection and intersection.[63]

For co-founder and then-Chairman of Global Business Network the Jewish Peter Schwartz, also writing in a prefatory letter in the document:

> The Rockefeller Foundation's use of scenario planning to explore technology and international development has been both inspired

---

[63] Rodin and Schwartz, *Scenarios for the Future*, 4.

and ambitious. Throughout my 40-plus-year career as a scenario planner, I have worked with many of the world's leading companies, governments, foundations, and nonprofits—and I know firsthand the power of the approach.[64]

The "futurist" Schwartz is now with Salesforce, has been a consultant for films such as *Minority Report,* and in 2007, Schwartz moderated a forum entitled "The Impact of Web 2.0 and Emerging Social Network Models" as part of the World Economic Forum. Running through potential future scenarios in a section titled "Lock Step":

In 2012, the pandemic that the world had been anticipating for years finally hit. Unlike 2009's H1N1, this new influenza strain . . . originat[ed] from wild geese. . . . The pandemic . . . had a deadly effect on economies: international mobility of both people and goods screeched to a halt, debilitating industries like tourism and breaking global supply chains. Even locally, normally bustling shops and office buildings sat empty for months, devoid of both employees and customers.[65]

Just a reminder, this is from May 2010. The "Lock Step" scenario continues:

During the pandemic, national leaders around the world flexed their authority and imposed airtight rules and restrictions, from the mandatory wearing of face masks to body-temperature checks at the entries to communal spaces like train stations and supermarkets. Even after the pandemic faded, this more authoritarian control and oversight of citizens and their activities stuck and even intensified. In order to protect themselves from the spread of increasingly global problems—from pandemics and transnational terrorism to environmental crises and rising poverty—leaders around the world took a firmer grip on power.

At first, the notion of a more controlled world gained wide acceptance and approval. Citizens willingly gave up some of their sovereignty—and their privacy—to more paternalistic states in

---

[64] Ibid., 6.
[65] Ibid., 18.

exchange for greater safety and stability. . . . [N]ational leaders had more latitude to impose order in the ways they saw fit. In developed countries, this heightened oversight took many forms: biometric IDs for all citizens, for example. . . .

China's investment in Africa expanded as the bargain of new jobs and infrastructure in exchange for access to key minerals or food exports proved agreeable to many governments. Cross-border ties proliferated in the form of official security aid. While the deployment of foreign security teams was welcomed in some of the most dire failed states, one-size-fits-all solutions yielded few positive results.

Technology trends and applications we might see: Scanners using advanced functional magnetic resonance imaging (fMRI) technology become the norm at airports and other public areas to detect abnormal behavior that may indicate "antisocial intent"; . . . Nations create their own independent, regionally defined IT networks, mimicking China's firewalls.[66]

And yet here they are, offering us one-size-fits-all solutions. Curious. Indeed, the desire to rub out all distinctions between and among people is a common theme with the ruling class. As Yuval Noah Harari wrote in *Sapiens: A Brief History of Humankind*, "Having close to 200 independent states is a hindrance rather than a help."[67] Better to be a node in a network, right? A fungible widget? Automation is perhaps the ultimate homogenizer—inorganic, artificial. And this is the false god the transhumanists have put their faith in.

Returning to the *Scenarios for the Future of Technology and International Development* document, more priming is apparent through the "Hack Attack" scenario, reminiscent of Cyber Polygon. In this scenario:

[M]ore sophisticated hackers attempted to take down corporations, government systems, and banks via phishing scams and database information heist. . . . Security measures and screenings tightened. . . . Verifying the authenticity of anything was increasingly difficult."[68]

---

[66] Ibid., 19, 21, 23.
[67] Harari, *Sapiens*, 224.
[68] Rodin and Schwartz, *Scenarios for the Future*, 36.

We also see the food connection once again, and a pretty clear nod to where the future appears to be headed:

> [T]he global have/have-not gap grew wider than ever. The very rich still had the financial means to protect themselves; gated communities sprung up from New York to Lagos, providing safe havens surrounded by slums. In 2025, it was de rigueur to build not a house but a high-walled fortress, guarded by armed personnel. The wealthy also capitalized on the loose regulatory environment to experiment with advanced medical treatments and other under-the-radar activities.
>
> Those who couldn't buy their way out of chaos—which was most people—retreated to whatever "safety" they could find. . . .
>
> The operational model in this world is a "fortress model" in which philanthropic organizations coalesce into a strong, single unit to combat fraud and lack of trust. . . .
>
> [S]ynthetic biology, often state-funded, is used to "grow" resources and foodstuffs that have become scarce.
>
> New threats like weaponized biological pathogens and destructive botnets dominate public attention. . . .
>
> Identity-verification technologies become a staple of daily life. . . .[69]

Now as I mentioned, there are these different plot lines that intersect with the virus, as the "elites" and their AI auto-generators don't just sculpt narratives but script them. One of which is climate change, which we will explore in more depth later, and another is the "double pandemic" of COVID-19 and white supremacy. To what in a sane world would be to its discredit, *Qualitative Social Work* published an article in March 2021 entitled "The Double Pandemic: COVID-19 and White Supremacy." Just like the all-too-familiar, recycled drivel you've likely heard a thousand times from the privileged mediocrities, in our universities, and on television, we learn that:

> The interconnectedness of the COVID-19 pandemic and the pandemic of racism (both anti-Black and anti-Asian) in 2020 have exacerbated inequalities and followed predictable historical pathways.

---

[69] Ibid., 37–39.

> *However, as most individuals from marginalized backgrounds*
> *know, the pandemic of racism is nothing new. It has been superim-*
> *posed on top of the pre-existing racism, xenophobia, blaming, and*
> *"othering." The common roots of all this lie in White supremacy.*

The author, Briana Starks, then goes on to explain that Black men don't like wearing masks because of "being characterized as criminal and hyper-policed"—well, go look at the FBI's crime statistics. Speaking of the FBI, this is contrasted with "White men storm[ing] the state capital of Michigan, to protest the infringement of their 'civil rights' after the state's governor implemented a state-wide mask mandate early in the pandemic." This plot was instigated by FBI informants. Laughable, but not a joke. To quote Mark Steyn:

> *You can laugh, but no one who matters is laughing.*
> *We now live in an age of state ideology. There's a correct posi-*
> *tion on certain subjects and it's an ever-growing list. . . .*
> *There's something ugly and tyrannous in the air. And I don't use*
> *that term lightly.*
> *Tyranny is always capricious, and you can fall afoul of it no*
> *matter how hard you try to keep up.*
> *A joke is the smallest indicator and most reliable indicator of*
> *liberty, so laugh it up while you can because there will be no jokes in*
> *the future, none, it will be a wasteland of plonking earnestness.*[70]

This is confirmed by the creation of the Disinformation Governance Board under the Department of Homeland Security, led by Nina Jankowicz, who does musical numbers on social media about "disinformation" and was apparently at one time performing "wizard rock" with erotic Harry Potter lyrics and political themes. According to her biography at the Wilson Center website, she "advised the Ukrainian government on strategic communications under the auspices of a Fulbright-Clinton Public Policy Fellowship." Also, "Prior to her Fulbright grant in Ukraine, Ms. Jankowicz managed democracy assistance programs to Russia and Belarus at the National Democratic Institute for International Affairs." The Jewish US Secretary of State Antony Blinken—one of the lead agitators for war with Russia, going so far

---

[70] Steyn, "You Can Laugh."

as to head to the Ukraine physically "to demonstrate the United States' un-wavering commitment to Ukraine and the Ukrainian people in their struggle against Russian aggression"—is on the Wilson Center's Board of Trustees. Jankowicz is your typical mid-thirties limp wrist who essentially lives online and only cares about her "career." Her book *How to be a Woman Online* is testament to that fact. I bet she orders through Uber Eats five times a week.

But living online—a vicarious no-life as it were—is *exactly* where the so-called "elites" want us, not in the real world doing real things and making real connections. This is anathema to the project, and if they can't addict you or brainwash you into thinking the digital sphere is anything other than a meeting place of sorts or a place of exchange (such as of ideas or commerce, an intermediary as it were), they'll try to make reality so awful that it seems the only respite. Even its intermediary aspects can often be an issue, as it can interfere with direct interaction and engagement, with nature or between people as examples.

Yet this warped idea of progress surges ever forward. Consider the UK's AI Council, "an independent expert committee, [which] provides advice to Government and high-level leadership of the Artificial Intelligence (AI) ecosystem." It is Chaired by Tabitha Goldstaub, UK AI Business Champion and co-founder of CogX, and features members such as Mark Walport (Formerly UKRI and Government's Chief Scientific Adviser), Chris Bishop (Microsoft Research Lab), Ann Cairns (MasterCard), Rachel Dunscombe (NHS Digital Academy—you might recall that the NHS has been a target of ransomware attacks in recent years; the NHS is a major customer of Darktrace), and Lila Ibrahim (DeepMind). Among the Council's roles is to "Increas[e] skills in AI, including the diversity of people studying and working in AI," because diversity is always our greatest strength, even when we're engineering the superintelligences of the future that may well enslave and/or exterminate us.

Another member of the AI Council is Nick Jennings, a member of the Advisory Board of Darktrace: "Founded in 2013 by mathematicians and cyber experts from government intelligence backgrounds, Darktrace was the first company to apply AI to the challenge of cyber security. With its Immune System platform, Darktrace has fundamentally transformed the ability of organizations to defend their most critical assets in the face of rising cyber-threat." Alongside Jennings on the Darktrace Advisory Council (with descriptions from the Darktrace website) we find the following:

Lord Evans was Director General of MI5 from 2007 to 2013. He spent 33 years with MI5, defending the UK against internal and domestic terrorism and cyber-threats. He was appointed to the Security Service's Management Board as Director of International Counter Terrorism in 2001, ten days before the 9/11 attacks on the World Trade Center. He was appointed to the House of Lords in 2014 at the personal recommendation of the Prime Minister and sits as a cross-bench peer. Lord Evans is also a non-executive Director of HSBC Holdings and of Ark Datacentres Ltd. . . .

Alan Wade had a thirty-five-year career in the Central Intelligence Agency, where he latterly served as the Chief Information Officer, before his retirement in 2005.[71] Prior to this role, Alan held a series of senior positions at the CIA, including the Director of Communications and Director of Security. . . .

After a career in banking, venture capital and head hunting, Amber Rudd became the MP for Hastings and Rye from 2010 to 2019. She held three cabinet roles over four years and under three Prime Ministers, first in Energy and Climate Change, then the Home Office as Home Secretary and until September 2019 in Work and Pensions. She also twice served as Minister for Women and Equalities. As Energy Secretary she steered the UK's participation in the crucial and successful Paris Climate Change Agreement in 2015. As Home Secretary she oversaw the UK's response to the terrorist attacks in 2017. Under her leadership the UK led on setting up an international industry-led response to removing radicalising material on the internet which endures as the Global Internet Forum to Counter Terrorism (GIFCT). She is now a Senior Advisor to Teneo, Management Consultants. She is also an Advisor to Pool Re, insurers for terrorism risk. She recently became a Trustee for The Climate Group, working with the private sector to reach a net zero outcome.

According to his Imperial College London biography, Jennings is the Vice-Provost for Research and Enterprise and Professor of Artificial Intelligence at Imperial College London. He is "an internationally-recognised authority in the areas of AI, autonomous systems, cyber-security and agent-based

---

[71] *Through a series of connections, Wade is a key figure in connecting a number of dots in a web including various Israeli firms, British and American intelligence, Facebook, and Peter Thiel/Palantir, among others.*

computing." He is a member of the governing body of the Engineering and Physical Sciences Research Council, the Monaco Digital Advisory Council, and chair of the Royal Academy of Engineering's Policy Committee. Before Imperial, Nick was the UK's first Regius Professor of Computer Science and the UK Government's first Chief Scientific Advisor for National Security. "Nick's personal research focuses on developing AI systems for large-scale, open and dynamic environments. In particular, he is interested in how to endow individual autonomous agents with the ability to act and interact in flexible ways and with effectively engineering systems that contain both humans and software agents." He is a Fellow of the Royal Academy of Engineering, the Institute of Electrical and Electronic Engineers, the British Computer Society, the Institution of Engineering and Technology, the Association for the Advancement of Artificial Intelligence (AAAI), the Society for the Study of Artificial Intelligence and Simulation of Behaviour (AISB), the Royal Society of the Arts, the City and Guilds of London Institute, the German AI Institute (DFKI), and the European Artificial Intelligence Association, and is a member of Academia Europaea. He is also involved with a number of start-ups including Aerogility, Crossword Cybersecurity, Contact Engine, Darktrace, Rebellion Defence, and Reliance Cyber Systems. Without going too far into the weeds—although to be fair the weeds are quite often where the action is—suffice it to say that the relevant organizations overlap in personnel and collaboration and span the university network as well as the military-industrial and medical-industrial complexes, logistics and transportation sectors, and everything in between. Illustrative is Aerogility, whose major clients include Lockheed Martin, BAE Systems, Rolls-Royce, EasyJet, Boeing, and Cranfield University. Alongside Jennings, co-Chief Scientific Advisor Michael Luck is Professor of Computer Science and Director of the UKRI Centre for Doctoral Training on Safe and Trusted Artificial Intelligence. Luck is also an AI Advisory Board member with Jennings at Contact Engine, which partners with companies such as Oracle, DHL, Microsoft, and Amdocs.

As a 2017 proposal from Wendy Hall (University of Southampton) and Jérôme Pesenti (Facebook AI) with the support of the Business Secretary and Culture Secretary and in consultation with the like of the City of London, DeepMind, Microsoft, and Pfizer outlines in the case of Great Britain:

We are at the threshold of an era when much of our productivity and prosperity will be derived from the systems and machines we create.

We are accustomed now to technology developing fast, but that pace will increase and AI will drive much of that acceleration. The impacts on society and the economy will be profound. . . .

Increased use of Artificial Intelligence (AI) can bring major social and economic benefits to the UK. With AI, computers can analyse and learn from information at higher accuracy and speed than humans can. AI offers massive gains in efficiency and performance to most or all industry sectors, from drug discovery to logistics. AI is software that can be integrated into existing processes, improving them, scaling them, and reducing their costs, by making or suggesting more accurate decisions through better use of information.[72]

This will, however, require the "need to increase ease of access to data in a wider range of sectors," and they recommend, apropos of nothing, "Greater diversity in the AI workforce." Their recommendations were largely accepted, and the report led to a "Sector Deal" aimed at solidifying partnerships between the government and the tech industry to "boost innovation in AI." As we might expect, all the 5G infrastructure and the like is present. The policy paper also states, "We are already home to some of the biggest names in the business such as Deepmind, Swiftkey and Babylon." Babylon is Babylon Health, partnered with the NHS, BuzzFeed, Shell, HSBC, and others. Babylon offers a digital healthcare app for "AI-powered diagnosis."

Additionally, the UK government does, in fact, have an Office for Artificial Intelligence, and, as Digital Secretary Oliver Dowden said in a March 2021 press release, "Unleashing the power of AI is a top priority in our plan to be the most pro-tech government ever." This is a government that, by the way, is helmed by a Conservative. For what it's worth, like Joe Biden's campaign to "Build Back Better"—gleaned straight from the World Economic Forum—the UK Conservatives' website loudly proclaims that they aim to "Build Back Better" as well.

It's not like Britain is alone, however, as many countries race to build up their AI capacities. From the vaunted multistakeholder perspective held by organizations such as the World Economic Forum, this is a very good thing. It's not so much a competition between countries, though it looks that way from the outside, as it is a race to provide more data sets and information to be plugged into the network and accelerate the project.

---

[72] Hall and Pesenti, Growing the Artificial Intelligence Industry, 1–2.

Have you ever noticed that outside of a very few quickly marginalized figures, no one in a position of authority ever seems to question the wisdom of any of this, outside, perhaps, of the late Tanzanian President John Magufuli who as a "COVID-19 skeptic" speculatively and all-too-conveniently died of "COVID-19-related complications"?

With COVID-19 as justification, as usual, the WEF noted in July 2020—recalling the Dataist obsession with the free flow of information—that, "By necessity, model-based AI (which leverages the data available) saw a resurgence. As the pandemic progressed, and more data was available, data-rich and model-free approaches could be combined, leading to a few key hybrid solutions." The pandemic, "provided an opportunity for data scientists and AI scientists to put their advanced techniques and tools to use by helping business leaders make decisions in a challenging environment that's dominated by speed, uncertainty and lack of data." This will "ensure you can seek solutions quickly while maximizing the technologies and processes already in place." [73] The same thought process, and the same emphasis on processes and systems already in place but situated to be scaled-up, includes the various medical interventions and global distribution of highly experimental mRNA "vaccines." As the same authors, Kay Firth-Butterfield (Head of Artificial Intelligence and Machine Learning; Member of the Executive Committee, World Economic Forum) and Anand Rao (Global Leader, Artificial Intelligence, PricewaterhouseCoopers) wrote in May 2020:

> *Data is critical to build models and validate their accuracy. . . . In the case of COVID-19, we need to feed models. . . .*
>
> *Models can be used to change the behaviour of people. We are all familiar with models that make recommendations as to which books we should read and what products we should buy. Similarly, COVID-19 models have changed attitudes and behaviours of health officials, policymakers, government institutions and citizens. . . .*
>
> *In response to government interventions, citizens have largely complied with restrictions and changed behaviours. They are traveling less, sheltering at home, social distancing and being more conscious of disinfection. They have also changed purchase behaviour. They are shopping online more rather than going to physical stores,*

---

[73] Rao and Firth-Butterfield, "3 Ways COVID-19."

and they are consuming more bandwidth as social interactions and entertainment have largely moved online.[74]

The World Economic Forum consciously links things like AI, nanotech, nuclear energy, and GMOs with quantum computing and the ethical use thereof. As we have seen in the effort to completely re-shape the human experience in record time, what is ethical by the WEF and their compatriots' definition is pretty far from what any normal, sane person would define as ethical. Nevertheless, whether it be biometric data or agriculture, it's all got to be brought under control and linked.

The World Economic Forum's New Vision for Agriculture features such partners as Monsanto, DuPont, Cargill, the Wellcome Trust, Walmart, the Rockefeller Foundation, and Unilever. Given the "gifts" we've gotten from Monsanto's GMO monstrosities and their destruction of sustainable agriculture and independent farms, DuPont's carcinogenic "forever chemicals," or the shoving of millions into overcrowded hovels and the degradation of the land and food quality courtesy of the Rockefeller Foundation's efforts in the twentieth century, these are decidedly *not* the people we want forming a new vision for agriculture, or anything for that matter. But agriculture, like everything else, must be made "smarter."

Thus, the World Economic Forum and its obsession with Smart Cities and a vast network encompassing everything from biometric data to trees in the park takes on a whole new light. With an impetus to "build back better," the WEF's Global Future Council on Cities of Tomorrow notes that they "will seek to identify how cities can be re-designed to build back better and provide the climate and resilience, social and digital infrastructure to do so." With partnering organizations such as Microsoft, Peking University, the Australian Smart Communities Association, Access Israel, Google, the Centre for Digital Built Britain, Asian Infrastructure Investment Bank, Columbia University, Bloomberg Associates, the Canada Infrastructure Bank, and the King Abdulaziz City for Science and Technology (KACST), the WEF's Future of Cities initiative encompasses the Global Future Council on Cities of Tomorrow, as well as Infrastructure 4.0, Net Zero Carbon Cities, and the G20 Global Smart Cities Alliance (note the constant inclusion of the buzzword "smart," which typically occurs in close proximity to others like "sustainable"—with the proposals anything but—and "clean").

---

[74] Rao and Firth-Butterfield, "Lessons from COVID-19."

The New Zealand Government is deeply enmeshed with the WEF's AI projects; as a June 2020 white paper from the World Economic Forum entitled "Reimaging Regulation for the Age of AI: New Zealand Pilot Project" informs:

A number of initiatives in New Zealand – such as the government's Algorithm Assessment Report, the Centre for AI and Public Policy, Otago University report, Government Use of AI in New Zealand, and the AI Forum of New Zealand's work on AI in the economy and society – have raised the importance of AI and explored opportunities. . . .

New Zealand has expressed interest in working with the Centre for the Fourth Industrial Revolution on this topic, given the need for a global, multistakeholder perspective on the complex question of regulating AI. New Zealand has been keen to work with the Centre to identify tools and approaches that would promote innovation, protect society and build trust in AI use. . . .

Also in New Zealand, the Data Futures Partnership framed social licence in 2017 as the acceptance by individuals for organizations to use their data, information and stories.[75]

According to the World Economic Forum's "Shaping the Future of Technology Governance: Artificial Intelligence and Machine Learning"—with partners including the New Zealand Government as well as Amazon, Lockheed Martin, Salesforce, the Government of Rwanda, Saudi Aramco, the Government of Azerbaijan, Palantir, Huawei, Microsoft, Facebook/Meta, Google, the Dubai Water and Electricity Authority, the Government of Serbia's Office for Information Technologies and e-Government, and JP Morgan Chase:

Artificial Intelligence (AI) is a key driver of the Fourth Industrial Revolution. Its effect can be seen in homes, businesses and even public spaces. In its embodied form of robots, it will soon be driving cars, stocking warehouses and caring for the young and elderly. AI holds the promise of solving some of society's most pressing issues, but

---

[75] Madzou, et al., "Reimagining Regulation," 5, 14.

also presents challenges such as inscrutable "black box" algorithms, unethical use of data and potential job displacement.

As rapid advances in machine learning (ML) increase the scope and scale of AI's deployment across all aspects of daily life, and as the technology can learn and change on its own, multistakeholder collaboration is required.

Of course, the stakeholders are already in place to provide the solutions to the problems they've created! Regarding the inscrutable black boxes specifically, Cynthia Rudin and Joanna Radin explicate in an article in *Harvard Data Science Review*:

In machine learning, these black box models are created directly from data by an algorithm, meaning that humans, even those who design them, cannot understand how variables are being combined to make predictions. Even if one has a list of the input variables, black box predictive models can be such complicated functions of the variables that no human can understand how the variables are jointly related to each other to reach a final prediction.

The existence of black box algorithms and self-perpetuating systems lends credence to the idea that the carefully calculated and scripted events we have seen play out over the past several years may well be driven by some sort of superintelligence that merely has humans doing its bidding. For Rudin and Radin, "Trusting a black box model"—trusting the science, as it were—"means that you trust not only the model's equations, but also the entire database that it was built from." You understand that there is no room for human sovereignty or biological integrity in such a model. For Juan Manuel Duran and Karin Rolanda Jongsma in an article in *Journal of Medical Ethics*, "By outlining that more transparency in algorithms is not always necessary, and by explaining that computational processes are indeed methodologically opaque to humans, we argue that the reliability of algorithms provides reasons for trusting the outcomes of medical artificial intelligence (AI)." Trust the numbers/data set (cough, COVID, cough) and the authorities. Shut up and obey.

The World Economic Forum's Platform for Shaping the Future of the Internet of Things and Urban Transformation states:

The COVID-19 pandemic has forced us to rethink the way we live. It is transforming industries and how we do business. It is intensifying social and environmental crises in our communities. And it is challenging fundamental assumptions and global trends. . . .

A growing suite of connected devices and smart technologies, commonly referred to as the internet of things (IoT), offers a means to reimagine and transform physical spaces—our homes, offices, factories, farms, healthcare facilities and public spaces.

COVID-19 forced none of this, but was a handy excuse to accelerate projects and proposals years in the making, in the same way that pressure for everyone to get the so-called "vaccine" represents the chance for a very large sample size to test mRNA modifications on, if not itself be the Trojan Horse to cause a mass die-off and get those pesky carbon emissions under control. Other possibilities include the uploading of more data sets into the expanding IoAT and a breaking-down of biological barriers to biotechnological mergers.

Indeed, were one to break down all of the barriers to getting everything online, you'd do worse than using the language of humanism to do it—the WEF's Future of the Connected World initiative lists "combatting inequality" alongside other essential actions, such as "improving security." In fact, their inherent neatness and seamlessness almost leads one to wonder if there is already a kind of superintelligence guiding the implementation of all of these systems that can and do operate independent of human intervention in many cases already—often needing only human inputs, which gives grim meaning to "human resources," does it not?

In a grotesque paradox, many of the most avowed liberal humanists such as Niall Ferguson cede human sovereignty to systems; is it such a stretch to go from *The Square and the Tower*'s premise that "Man, with his unrivaled neural network, was born *to* network" to Man actually *becoming* the network? Reflect on the social network that is Facebook, for example, and consider the role of data in its expanding AI efforts. How many people basically already live online? For Stuart Montgomery of the *Tufts Observer*, "One of the most common iterations of machine learning in use today is called a 'neural network,' because it takes its basic metaphorical structure from the brain." After all, all processes are reducible to algorithms to follow Yuval Noah Harari's logic—a logic, it should be noted, that is widely held by many a Dataist. Glenn Zorpette, in "Waiting for the Rapture," writes:

> *Consciousness seems mystical and inextricably linked to organisms. What happens in the cerebral cortex that turns objective information into subjective experience? We don't know, but we will someday. No one argues that consciousness arises from anything but biological processes in the brain. The brain is a computer.*

Crucially, for Harari and synching with Ferguson:

> *Every day I absorb countless data . . . and transmit back new bits. . . . I don't really know where I fit into the greater scheme of things. . . . This relentless flow of data sparks new inventions and disruptions that nobody plans, controls or comprehends. . . . No one needs to understand. All you need to do is answer your emails faster—and allow the system to read them. . . . As the global data-processing system becomes all-knowing and all-powerful, so connecting to the system becomes the source of all meaning.*[76]

In this way we can see the utter reliance of humans on the systems they've constructed, *not* the other way around. Rather than gods, humans have made themselves into slaves, serving the system and becoming just more data sets in the process. As Harari continues, "Dataism isn't anti-humanist. It has nothing against human experiences. It just doesn't think they are intrinsically valuable."[77] It is not a stretch here to go from the worthlessness of human experiences to the worthlessness of humans.

Our extinction in one possible scenario is simply a by-product. For Gordon Bell of Microsoft Research, "Singularity is that point in time when computing is able to know all human and natural-systems knowledge and exceed it in problem-solving capability with the diminished need for humankind as we know it. I basically support the notion."[78] In trying to upgrade humanity, Harari concedes it "may not be enough" and that humanity may well need to be "retired." This is should we continue on the current trajectory, and the entirety of the so-called "elites" are committed to doing

---

[76] Harari, *Homo Deus*, Chapter 11.
[77] Ibid.
[78] Quoted in *IEEE Spectrum* (June 2008).

just that, whether they are Dataists, techno-humanists, power-mad socio-paths, or servile functionaries (or some combination thereof).

A slightly different point of view is held by John Casti of the International Institute for Applied Systems Analysis in Austria, a designer of computer simulations of complex human systems, like the stock market, highway traffic, and the insurance industry:

> *I think [the singularity is] scientifically and philosophically on sound footing. The only real issue for me is the time frame over which the singularity will unfold. [The singularity represents] the end of the supremacy of Homo sapiens as the dominant species on planet Earth. At that point a new species appears, and humans and machines will go their separate ways.*[79]

Though Casti does not believe this implies machines or superintelligences annihilating humans ("unless human interests start to interfere with those of the machines"), it is telling that he cites the relationship of humans with bees—whom we exploit for resources and to whom we are societally indifferent to their declining populations as we wreak havoc on the environment.

Vernor Vinge considers a variety of possible outcomes:

> *In my 1993 essay, "The Coming Technological Singularity," I said I'd be surprised if the singularity had not happened by 2030. I'll stand by that claim, assuming we avoid showstopping catastrophes.*
>
> *I expect the singularity will come as some combination of the following:*
> - *The AI Scenario: We create superhuman artificial intelligence (AI) in computers.*
> - *The IA Scenario: We enhance human intelligence through human-to-computer interfaces to achieve intelligence amplification (IA).*
> - *The Biomedical Scenario: We directly increase our intelligence by improving the neurological operation of our brains.*

---

[79] Ibid.

- *The Internet Scenario: Humanity, its networks, computers, and databases become sufficiently effective to be considered a superhuman being.*
- *The Digital Gaia Scenario: The network of embedded microprocessors becomes sufficiently effective to be considered a superhuman being.*[80]

If you know your Ted Kaczynski, your *Doctor Faustus*, or your scripture, you know where this is going and, indeed, where it is originating from.

Understanding that many aspects of this topic require the reader to go out on quite a limb, at bare minimum, whether they believe them or not, the zealots of Dataism, just the same as the zealots of communism or "social justice," do believe in what they're preaching and doing with religious fervor. It is worth recalling that there was a slight possibility that the Trinity tests of the Manhattan Project could ignite the atmosphere, but they went ahead anyway. This naturally begs the question: will you "follow the science" to oblivion or will you choose a different path? Let's look further ahead down this one, though, at the justifications that will be used to paint you into a corner—such as "climate change" and the knee-capping of industry and agriculture, as when, for example, the Dutch government pledged to curtail nitrogen emissions by up to 70% by 2030 to "save nature and make the construction of houses possible," effectively crippling the country's agricultural sector, one of the most productive in the world—and manufacture "solutions" to artificially-created problems.

---

[80] Vinge, "Signs of the Singularity."

Chapter Five:
Climate Change, the Food Supply, and Enthusiastic Eugenicists

"I'd rather die with a burger in my colon than live and eat faux-fu."
–Hank Hill

2030 has become almost this mythical endpoint for all of the various globalist projects such as the United Nations' 2030 Agenda for Sustainable Development and the World Economic Forum's 2030Vision. For what it's worth, the latter project's partners include Salesforce, Amazon, Google, Facebook, two arms of the United Nations, the Government of Botswana, Microsoft, Amazon, the Overseas Development Institute (a kind of Chatham House/USAID-type entity), and more. This 2030 vision is reflected pretty much across the board of most all globalist institutions (irrespective of "public" or "private"), from the aforementioned lot to the Government of Saudi Arabia ("Vision2030") to the World Health Organization's Immunization Agenda 2030.

The planning has long been in the works, and the infrastructure and regulatory framework is being brought online as we speak. The globalist network must be understood in the context of this transhumanist project. Although perhaps not even all senior leadership is on board with this particular vision, it *is* the prevailing vision of those who are implementing autonomous systems, using high-energy particle physics (CERN) to try to unlock sub-atomic secrets, and driving the quantum-computing explosion and the proliferation of the infrastructure to support the IoAT. The talk about "sustainability" and "combatting inequality" is just co-opted humanist drivel; admittedly, many people preaching and practicing this globalist vision believe in these ideals, but they are a means to an end. These people are disposable assets, and in any revolution, they are usually the first to go.

These ultra-sonic, super-city people of tomorrow with their seventeen booster shots love the idea of infinity Congolese in *your* neighborhood and crushing all dissent through censorship and worse, all while wearing the happy face of liberalism. It's pathetic, it's laughable, but it's proving terribly effective in social norm policing in many areas, particularly the cities and suburbs. These are the same people who think you can't get COVID if you're out protesting for racial justice, in the same way you can't get it if you're sitting down at a restaurant; nor can you get it from someone who crossed the border illegally. "Hate has no home here" the sign proclaims on their well-manicured lawn, cut by Hector from Honduras who's doing the work the teenager on TikTok down the road won't do. Now to be fair, there's actually a decent-sized nugget of truth here, but this state of affairs has been artificially created, like everything else with this agenda, over a long period of indoctrination and frankly classism. The end result are people like Jen Psaki and Nina Jankowicz with no useful skills or functional ability to survive.

This is precisely why we see the war on those who would produce their own inputs, especially through agriculture. Whether it's banning the sale of chickens or the collection of rainwater, there is wide-spread institutional support geared toward removing the ability of people to provide for themselves. This pressure to snuff out self-reliance takes a variety of forms, from the international to the local. Everything must be brought under the control of one central authority who will then dictate what you get and how much, if anything. If it sounds a whole lot like communism, that's because it is—but remember, communism in application more often than not gets its start-up money from high finance the same way these artificial intelligence companies do. And why not? Everything must be linked and interconnected, as we are seeing.

A Canadian woman was recently the first to officially receive a medical diagnosis of "suffering from climate change," and seemingly every major institution on board with the globalist agenda—from Carnegie Europe ("What the COVID-19 Pandemic Tells Us About Climate Change and Diplomacy") to Harvard ("Coronavirus, Climate Change, and the Environment: A Conversation on COVID-19 with Dr. Aaron Bernstein, Director of

Harvard Chan C-CHANGE") to the World Bank ("COVID-19 Responses Could Help Fight Climate Change")—has come out with some word-salad connecting COVID-19 and climate change. They were all of course delighted that carbon emissions went down since no one could go anywhere, tied to their land or even better someone else's like modern-day serfs. Even our Great Reset overlords at the World Economic Forum lament that "Nearly half of the respondents from a global survey do not understand the link between climate change and infectious diseases such as COVID-19." This clearly illustrates that any and all rhetorical and narrative means are being used to get as many people on board with the project as possible before turning to more coercive methods. We are in the midst of fifth generation warfare, a concept I will explicate more fully later; for now, we will continue to consider the soft power implications and the larger trends that suggest and even explicitly state in many cases where we are being led.

Writing for the *MIT Sloan Management Review* in 2019, Andrew S. Winston discussed the "mega-trends" the "elites" have in store for the global population in 2030, which include at least two-thirds of the world's projected 8.5 billion people shoved into cities, where "effects will include the need for more big buildings with better management technologies (big data and AI that makes buildings much more efficient)." Additionally, Winston writes:

> The amount of information collected on every person, product, and organization will grow exponentially, and the pressure to share that information — with customers and consumers in particular — will expand. . . . But all these tools will shatter privacy in the process.

Technology is clearly the accelerant toward this globalist Panopticon, whatever the justification, be it climate change, "inclusion," or COVID-19 contact tracing and vaccine passports, which are already being tied to financial services, such as Samsung Pay and CommonHealth's Vaccine Pass, "a digital version of your COVID-19 vaccine record you can conveniently add to Samsung Pay." Other similar apps include CLEAR Health Pass (by the way, CLEAR Health Pass's catchphrase is "Come Back Better") and Excelsior Pass. Why would this be necessary? And think longer-term, not the short-term justifications.

In *The Fourth Industrial Revolution*, Klaus Schwab also explicitly outlines the three megatrends of the Fourth Industrial Revolution as physical, digital, and biological. Via Jeff Merritt, Head of IoT, Robotics and Smart Cities for the World Economic Forum, Center for the Fourth Industrial Revolution, "Our research on hundreds of IoT implementations showed that 84 percent of them directly addressed, or had the potential to address, UN Sustainable Development Goals."[81] The United Nations is a very useful vehicle, especially if for Dataists the unrestricted flow of information in ever-increasing velocity—like goods, capital, and labor for globalist neoliberals before them—is viewed as the central pillar of their religion. We know that the World Economic Forum and the United Nations signed a Strategic Partnership Framework outlining areas of cooperation to "deepen institutional engagement and jointly accelerate the implementation of the 2030 Agenda for Sustainable Development." The Strategic Partnership Framework, signed in June 2019, focuses on the areas of not just financing the 2030 Agenda, but also on digital cooperation, health, education and skills, gender equality and the empowerment of women, and climate change. As the UN Secretary-General's *Roadmap for Financing the 2030 Agenda for Sustainable Development* outlines:

> *The 2030 Agenda, with its 17 Sustainable Development Goals (SDGs) and the Paris Agreement on climate change provide a pathway for a more prosperous, equitable and sustainable future. The Addis Ababa Action Agenda (AAAA) establishes a blueprint to support the implementation of the 2030 Agenda by providing a global framework for financing sustainable development that aligns all financing flows and policies with economic, social and environmental priorities. . . . The upcoming 'decade of action' (2020 – 2030) requires significant public and private investment to bring the SDGs and goals of the Paris Agreement to life for all people, everywhere.[82]*

In other words, creating a fully-integrated global network. While Harari claims that the "relentless flow of data sparks new inventions and disruptions that nobody plans, controls or comprehends,"[83] that's not entirely accurate, at least at this juncture (unless, as some have surmised, a

---

[81] Interviewed in Engelhardt, "'IoT improves.'"
[82] United Nations Secretary-General, *Roadmap for Financing*, 1.
[83] Harari, *Homo Deus*, Chapter 11.

superintelligence guiding events has already been brought online—a superintelligence that, theologically, could represent a downright sinister inhabitation).

The "end-to-end digital enabling infrastructure" being pushed by the World Economic Forum and its adherents will also encompass blockchain that will be tied to biometric data and social credit scores (thanks Chicoms!) in the new "smart," cashless, and "open" society where everywhere is nowhere. In this void of meaninglessness, the new data religion and the techno-humanist religion have supplanted what, for Harari and his ilk, are the quaint fictions of scripture. Without any proof beyond that "science" hasn't discovered the existence of souls, the modern Sadducee/Sophist Harari states that instead humanity is turning its gaze to what may well spell the death of liberalism in the form of the quest for immortality, happiness, and divinity. If the middle item on humanity's "new agenda" looks a lot like *Brave New World*, well, sometimes life imitates art. That or Aldous Huxley, whose brother Julian was a eugenicist, knew a thing or two about where this project was headed nearly a century ago.

Julian Huxley—the first Director-General of UNESCO, President of the British Eugenics Society, President of the British Humanist Association, and a founding member of the World Wildlife Fund—is commonly credited as the founder of transhumanism. Readers of *The Transgender-Industrial Complex* will note that the World Wildlife Fund is, despite its seeming innocuousness, deeply enmeshed in the globalist agenda (we will circle back around to a key aspect shortly). Of course, UNESCO is as well: the Moroccan-Jewish Audrey Azoulay, Director-General of UNESCO, states in "Towards an Ethics of Artificial Intelligence" in the *UN Chronicle* that developments in AI are relevant to every aspect of UNESCO's mandate, and that "AI could open up tremendous opportunities for achieving the Sustainable Development Goals (SDGs) set by the United Nations in the 2030 Agenda for Sustainable Development." The World Economic Forum announced its 2030Vision project under the auspices of the Centre for Nature and Climate; via their website, 2030Vision began as:

> A newly formed integration merging the 2030Vision Partnership Initiative launched by Arm in December 2017 with the Frontier 2030 initiative launched by the World Economic Forum in January 2020. The new initiative, 2030Vision is co-owned and developed with founding partners and co-chaired by Simon Segars, CEO, Arm and

Achim Steiner, Administrator, United Nations Development Programme (UNDP). 2030Vision aims to be the global public-private platform that puts the expertise and resources of the tech sector in service of accelerating the achievement of the Global Goals. The platform mobilizes technology companies, government, civil society and international organisation leaders to harness emerging technologies and at scale to accelerate action to achieve the Global Goals within the next decade. The platform seeks to form 4IR [Fourth Industrial Revolution] technology partnerships.

Arm's current CEO Rene Haas is also on the Board of Directors of yet another AI company, Mythic.

In some ways the World Economic Forum's obsession with digitization is a good thing, as their entire website features linkages and graphics outlining the various networks and how they intersect. This is highly useful for many reasons and shows in stark visual detail how exactly they are trying to shoehorn humanity into programmable "realities." Strategic planning and war gaming scenarios allow the ruling class to try to predict outcomes, aided in their endeavors by evermore powerful artificial intelligence and algorithms. They then craft a narrative to pre-plan our behavior and focus it where they need it to go. Consider Vasee Moorthy of the World Health Organization writing for the World Economic Forum in August 2020: "Back-casting is a method to work backwards from alternative future scenarios, and determine actions which can be taken now that influence which scenario comes to pass." So it is less about "preparedness" and more about trying to fix outcomes. This makes the kabuki theater of "democracy" all the more obvious once you understand that. You don't have a say, but it is important for the power structure that you *believe* that you do. It's why the Trojan Horse of liberalism has been so devastatingly effective in advancing this agenda, particularly when vague notions of "progress" all become conflated, where endless technological interventions and intermediaries, unnecessary and completely harmful layers of complexity and bureaucratic proceduralism are married to social progressivism, in the degenerate sense of "abortions for all!" and the like.

The pre-scripting and war gaming aspect is essential to understand; we can look at Event 201, for example, or its predecessor Clade X, where the unleashing of a global pandemic was war gamed and some might argue pre-planned. Perhaps, or perhaps it was opportunism. In either case, the infrastructure and the response were already in place. Were our leaders not sadistic degraded freaks, it would be reassuring that they've developed contingencies and strategies should something terrible happen. Since they are, it is not, especially as we've seen how many terrible situations we've been engineered into, not out of.

This also applies to the global supply chain particularly with regards to food and food security. In December 2015, the Center for American Progress, the World Wildlife Fund, Cargill, Mars, and CNA:

> *Developed and executed a policy decision-making game designed to explore issues arising from, and possible responses to, global food system disruptions. The game took place in November 2015 in Washington, D.C., and included senior officials and subject matter experts on teams representing Brazil, Continental Africa, China, the European Union (EU), India, the United States, Multilateral Institutions, and Business and Investors. During four rounds of game play spanning the decade 2020 to 2030, players confronted food system pressure at the intersection of population growth, urbanization, severe weather, and social unrest. In response, players crafted policies, made decisions, and took actions that dynamically influenced the state of the world as the game advanced. As the chain reaction of impacts tied to their choices became apparent, players experienced first-hand how their decisions and actions influenced global food security.*[84]

I won't go into too much depth about the players here—the reader is instructed to refer to *The Transgender-Industrial Complex* for additional context—other than to say that it's more of the usual suspects, headlined by the neo-liberal think tank the Center for American Progress (CAP). CAP's President is former Open Society Foundations President Patrick Gaspard, and it was founded by none other than John Podesta, who among other things was a representative to the UN High-Level Panel on the Post-2015 Development Agenda, the framework of which became the Sustainable Development Goals. According to an *MIT Press* blog post from 2017:

---

[84] Fisher and Su, *Food Chain Reactions*, iii.

> *Tony Podesta showed up in a wikileaks stash. In the email, [Marina] Abramovic invited Podesta's brother John . . . to join them at a "Spirit Cooking" dinner in her apartment in New York. . . .*
>
> *For the record: Spirit Cooking is nothing but a little-known (and, measured in her ouvre, a rather throwaway) performance Abramovic did in an Italian gallery in 1996, in which she painted apparent instructions on the white wall with pigs blood. Instructions like: "with a sharp knife cut deeply into the middle finger of your left hand eat the pain." She also painted a small kind of icon in the corner with the blood too. It's pretty repulsive and rather luridly aims to shock but it's also clearly not serious. Abramovic also published a Spirit Cooking cookbook, containing comico-mystical, self-helpy instructions like: "spit inside your naval / until the lake is filled / lie motionless / listen to the heartbeat / of a dog." You're not really meant to actually do these things. . . .*
>
> *Having known Marina for fourteen years now, and having written a biography, I don't think she's ever actually worshipped anything. . . . She essentially takes the spiritual and squeezes it into the purely bodily. . . . She kind of believes in everything—and therefore, in a way, in nothing. Except the power of the body.*

In other words, she and her cohort are the perfect embodiment of the ruling class as it were. Abramovic has publicly bragged about her three abortions, adding that in addition to this sacrifice to Moloch, having children would have been a "disaster for her work." As delightful as it would be to continue to explore the work of Marina Abramovic, we aren't quite finished with Podesta's Center for American Progress treating the lives and livelihoods of people as a game.

In July 2008, the Center for a New American Security (CNAS), with a consortium of ten partner organizations, hosted "Clout and Climate Change," an international climate change "war game" to explore the national security implications of global climate change. Some of these organizations included the Center for American Progress, Oak Ridge National Laboratory, McKinsey, the Brookings Institution, and the Rockefeller Brothers Fund. Some of the participants in the "game" featured representatives of the Gates Foundation, USAID, Refugees International, the US Army War College, the German Green Party, the United Nations Foundation, Harvard, Lockheed Martin, the Council on Foreign Relations,

Standard Chartered Bank, China Institutes of Contemporary International Relations (CICIR), and the Chinese Academy of Social Sciences. The scenario, set in a then-futuristic 2015, had:

> [F]our teams representing China, the European Union, India, and the United States, which are gathering in a special summit to examine climate change challenges that entail a high risk of conflict and to explore the possibilities for international cooperation. The rationale for bringing together only these four players (China, the EU, India, and the United States) is that these nations will be instrumental to future progress in cutting greenhouse gas emissions and adapting to the effects of global climate change. Other nations will play important roles, of course, but the game's designers made a judgment that the dynamics among these four players will be particularly important to explore and understand. . . .
>
> Two additional groups are essential to game play. First, an International Team will represent stakeholders (e.g., Japan, Russia, Brazil) that would be key to any international agreement on climate change. Although the International Team will not be a proactive player in the game, Country Teams may consult or negotiate with this team. Second, over the course of the game, ad hoc Issue Teams comprised of members from some or all Country Teams will be established to focus on issues expected to include resource scarcity, migration, disasters, and reduction of greenhouse gas emissions.[85]

The Center for a New American Security is yet another of these neo-liberal think tanks. Some of their major donors include: the MacArthur Foundation, Open Philanthropy, Facebook, Google, Amazon, the Carnegie Corporation of New York, Palantir, the Rockefeller Brothers Fund, Northrop Grumman, Raytheon, Lockheed Martin, JP Morgan Chase, Visa, UK Ministry of Defence, US Office of the Director of National Intelligence, the European Union (through the German Marshall Fund of the United States), the US State Department, Japan Bank for International Cooperation, the US Department of Defense, Deloitte, and the Open Society Foundations.

---

[85] Burke and Parthemore, eds., *Clout and Climate Change*, 17, 21.

Another representative organization, in this instance linking finance and "inclusion" (unless, presumably, you don't take the jab) would be the Council for Inclusive Capitalism established by the Vatican; according to its website, "The Council is led by Guardian CEOs and global leaders," who naturally include people like Marc Benioff of Salesforce, Mark Carney (UN Special Envoy for Climate Action and Finance and Prime Minister Boris Johnson's Finance Adviser for COP26; former Governor of the Bank of England; former Governor of the Bank of Canada; Board member of Bloomberg Philanthropies; member of the Group of Thirty; member of the Foundation Board of the World Economic Forum), William Lauder of the Estée Lauder Companies, Alex Gorsky of Johnson & Johnson, Kenneth C. Frazier of Merck, Mark Weinberger of EY, Darren Walker of the Ford Foundation, Rajiv Shah of the Rockefeller Foundation, and Lynn Forester de Rothschild (Inclusive Capital Partners, Estée Lauder Companies, Columbia University, E.L. Rothschild LLC, The Economist Group, Gulfstream, General Instruments, United Nations Advisory Committee on Inclusive Financial Services, the McCain Institute for International Leadership, National Information Infrastructure Advisory Committee and the Secretary of Energy Advisory Board under President Clinton, the Council on Foreign Relations, Bronfman-Rothschild, Chatham House). Other organizational partners include State Street, BP, Mastercard, Bank of America, TIAA, the OECD, Visa, DuPont, and the Office of the California State Treasurer.

Each of these organizations has made commitments that they explicitly align with select UN 2030 Agenda for Sustainable Development Goals. For example, Johnson & Johnson, producer of one of the major COVID-19 vaccines, declares that "the Millennium Goals were primarily the domain of governments. To achieve the even higher ambitions of the SDGs, the UN calls on all global citizens to take action. This includes us, the employees of Johnson & Johnson. As a globally operating company we take our responsibility and contribute in different areas. Johnson & Johnson focuses on SDG's 3, 5 and 17." Johnson & Johnson includes the production of vaccines for COVID-19 and HIV among those that align with the SDGs.

The insistence on vaccination for COVID-19 as the only option, with every major institution not just in the United States but across the globe putting enormous pressure on people to take it and in many cases mandate it even, is, to put it mildly, rather curious.

The United Nations states on its Sustainable Development Goals website that its SDGs not only intersect with climate change, but that "more important than ever, the goals provide a critical framework for COVID-19 recovery." In Klaus Schwab and Thierry Malleret's 2020 book *COVID-19: The Great Reset*, "recovery" from the pandemic—which they state "will not be possible without a vaccine"—is also explicitly tied to things like climate change. For Schwab and Malleret:

> Put simply: 'The Black Death may have been the unrecognized be-
> ginning of modern man.' If such profound social, political and eco-
> nomic changes could be provoked by the plague in the medieval
> world, could the COVID-19 pandemic mark the onset of a similar
> turning point with long-lasting and dramatic consequences for our
> world today?[86]

So again, whether COVID was intentionally released or not, and whether it was designed for lethality or not, it *is* being treated as a catalyzing event, the likes of which has been gamed-out well ahead of time. And with no piles of bodies, the propaganda machine has done an incredible job of keeping people in a perpetual state of panic and fear—and we know that fear is one of the great methods of control.

Sculpting narratives is a central feature of fifth generation warfare, a largely non-kinetic way of waging war centering on misinformation and information control, shaping of public and private perceptions, cyberat-tacks, and social engineering, with artificial intelligence and fully autono-mous systems as central to conducting said warfare. For True Believer Yu-val Noah Harari in an interview conducted by Alexis Papachelas:

> [H]umans think in stories, not in numbers. You need a good story.
> And it's difficult because the truth is far more complicated and pain-
> ful than the fictions. When you tell a completely fictional story you
> can tell a story that is simple. You can flatter people and they will
> like it. . . .
>
> In the 21st century, to make a country a colony, you don't need
> to send the tanks in. You just need to take the data out. We are now
> seeing a new form of imperialism – you can call it "data colonialism".
> It is all about the data.

---

[86] Schwab and Malleret, *COVID-19: The Great Reset*, Introduction.

In many ways, we can see the theater-level war in the Ukraine as a meeting of old school kinetic war from the Russian side, meeting a combination of fourth and fifth generation warfare on the Ukrainian side, with the Ukraine being treated as a proxy for the globalist technocratic state. Whether Russia is knowingly playing the villain under Putin as part of the global dialectic is unknown, but it is a real possibility worth considering.

Klaus Schwab (who literally has a book called *The Great Narrative* about COVID-19, "fake news," and "the way forward" released in 2022) has discussed the possibility of AI-shaping narratives, and given the number of sheer coincidences (or not), and the fact that AI does in fact now generate a significant number of news features as opposed to articles by human authors, this is not all that much of a stretch, especially given the advances in quantum computing. With velocity as a key feature of the modern world, as Schwab is quick to acknowledge, the power of AI to simply overwhelm the human mind in a deluge of data is becoming more of a possibility than ever. Indeed, as Harari states in his interview:

> [W]hen power is concentrated and hierarchical and you inject AI, it's much easier for algorithms to take it over. It's a gradual shift. More and more decisions are taken by the algorithms that humans don't understand. They trust their algorithm but they don't understand the decisions they are taking and they find increasingly that they become like puppets in the hands of these algorithms. And this can happen to China far quicker than the US because it is so centralized.

Despite the rhetoric about the defense of the Ukraine being about democracy, it is of course not; the corrupt Volodymyr Zelenskyy is precisely the kind of puppet the "democracies" want as a proxy. Though Harari believes that control via AI is more difficult in democracies due to the diffusion of power, there are no true democracies that have not been coopted or undermined with the window dressing of elections hiding the predetermined outcomes. The power is just as centralized, and of course he knows this; he's playing the game. The question is to what degree is artificial intelligence (or the demon in the machine if you like) already driving the people in power as opposed to simply being used as a tool? Are they unwittingly being manipulated by forces more powerful than they, and are they simply giving obedience to these forces as though they were gods in their own right? For Harari:

> *We are used to thinking of human life as a drama of decision making. Every great work of art, let's take ancient Greek drama, is about making a decision. Antigone is making a decision, Oedipus is making a decision. Now what happens in a world when increasingly all decisions are taken by an algorithm that knows you better? Increasingly the algorithm tells you what books to read, what films to watch, what to study, whom to marry, where to live. And we don't have any philosophical models for understanding such a life. What does it mean to live such a life when all your life is managed by these outside systems?*

We're already seeing the results: it means nothing if you believe in nothing, if you believe that you have no agency or have subconsciously surrendered to meaninglessness. So you extract what pleasures you can, navel-gazingly and narcissistically searching for validation in the void. Or you wallow in despair, doing the same. Or you surrender and pledge yourself to the machine, as Harari and other zealots like him have. They are in some ways like the character Cypher in *The Matrix*. Maybe Harari is right—there is a grand narrative, and meaning is where we see ourselves in the story. After all, as Shakespeare wrote, "All the world's a stage."

But Harari is wrong in one crucial way: the story isn't an arbitrary one like the sex you were assigned at birth (I'm joking about that last part). There is a grand cosmic drama to which we are a party, somehow, but of which we only get rare glimpses. "Science" as the transhumanists have constructed it illuminates nothing—it only obscures. One might even say it is Luciferian. Lucifer, or "Light Bringer," thrives on deception and false promises. It was the Enlightenment and the Scientific Revolution that brought us out of the so-called Dark Ages of superstition, was it not? And what is the central "superstition" we've been led away from? Interestingly, both promise to reveal objective truths, the secrets of our universe, and even everlasting life, but like Highlander, there can be only one. This is not to say that we should be rejecting the entire discipline of science out of hand or not using our intellects to better understand the world, cure diseases (not create new ones), and improve our quality of life. It *is* to say that unlike the world of algorithms Harari is working to create that robs humans of autonomy, you *do* have free will and you can make a decision where you place your faith—and this faith need not be blind.

If you believe—and contrary to what Harari states it's a matter of faith not science—that we have no souls and this life is all there is—then what Harari and company are selling might be appealing. As Harari explicates, intersecting with secular humanism and liberalism, for the techno-humanists:

> *The Universal Declaration of Human Rights does not say that humans have 'the right to life until the age of ninety'. It says that every human has a right to life, period. . . . An increasing minority of scientists and thinkers consequently . . . state that the flagship enterprise of modern science is to defeat death and grant humans eternal youth.*[87]

In reality, this quest for the Fountain of Youth is a devil's bargain humans have tried to make as long as our collective memories stretch—and probably much further. We see here the threads that could quite possibly come unraveled, however, as scientific humanism gives way to scientism, or the data religion, with systems, algorithms, and quantum computers as the golems of these would-be gods. But they cannot truly create, for only the Most High can do that. Instead, people like Elon Musk—despite his dire warnings about artificial intelligence, possessing the hubris to think that somehow we can control intelligences vastly more, well, intelligent than us—and Peter Thiel drive us ever-forward toward what might well spell our doom. I cannot emphasize this enough: this project is *the* existential threat we face, not some manufactured nonsense like "climate change."

Nevertheless, the currents of this global hive/Internet of Things project seem to be getting stronger, and they're taking us into some deep, threatening waters. With COVID-19 as justification and catalyst, we see all of the pieces falling neatly into place to realize the culmination of said project, racing headlong toward the mythical year of 2030. Parties and governments intertwined in this globalist network treat the UN's 2030 SDGs as binding. For example, Canada's Green Party, currently helmed by Annamie

---

[87] Harari, *Homo Deus*, Chapter 1.

Paul (described as "the first Black Canadian and first Jewish woman to be elected leader of a major federal party in Canada"), believes that the SDGs and the "climate emergency must be the lens through which every policy envelope is viewed–the economy, health, education, foreign affairs, immigration, public safety, defence, social welfare, transportation." Their actions support their words. According to Canada's Voluntary National Review submitted to the United Nations in 2018:

> *Canada is responding to these challenges through concrete actions to reduce poverty, advance gender equality and the empowerment of women and girls, narrow the socio-economic gaps that exist between different groups, foster inclusion and celebrate diversity, and improve equality of opportunity for all. . . .*
>
> *In June 2017, Canada announced its Feminist International Assistance Policy, which seeks to eradicate poverty and build a more peaceful, inclusive and prosperous world. Canada firmly believes that promoting gender equality and empowering women and girls is the most effective way to achieve this goal and drive progress on all SDGs. . . .*
>
> *The Government of Canada's policies, programs and priorities are already well-aligned to the SDGs. . . . Canada will mainstream a gender-responsive perspective in the implementation of the SDGs, consistent with its emphasis on gender equality as a cross-cutting priority.*
>
> *The Government of Canada will launch a process . . . to develop a national strategy on the 2030 Agenda through collaboration with all levels of government, Indigenous peoples, civil society and the private sector. Data is key to developing solutions to challenges facing the implementation of this Agenda, to ensure no one is left behind, and to track progress on the SDGs. As such, this report includes validated Canadian data for the SDG Global Indicator Framework.*[88]

Data being the "fossil fuel" of the Fourth Industrial Revolution as the digitized sphere becomes the focal point, moving away from the physical world and, as Schwab and Malleret note, *modifying* the physical realm:

---

[88] Government of Canada, *Canada's Implementation*, 2–3.

> *During the peak of the pandemic, O2O—online to offline—gained major traction. . . . This phenomenon of blurring the distinction between online and offline . . . has emerged as one of the most potent trends of the post-COVID-19 era. The pandemic crisis accelerated this phenomenon of eversion because it both forced and encouraged us towards a digital, "weightless" world faster than ever, as more and more economic activity had no choice but to take place digitally. . . . We could go as far as to say that, for a little while, teleportation supplanted transportation. . . . Large online companies like Amazon and Alibaba expanded decisively in the O2O business, particularly in food retailing and logistics.* [89]

The globalist Establishment has been working for some time to consolidate control over the food supply, as with everything else. As just one example of the current efforts, the Rockefeller Foundation has called for a need to "reimagine and re-design our food systems" as COVID-19 has been a "stress test" that somehow (this is never actually explicated by the Establishment even though they are constantly linking it) is connected to/exacerbates/comes from "climate change." Interesting that they admit this, but according to Sara Scherr (President and CEO of EcoAgriculture Partners) and Sara Farley (Managing Director, Integrated Operations, Food Initiative at the Rockefeller Foundation) writing for the World Economic Forum website on June 9th, 2020:

> *Today we see farmers dumping milk and ploughing crops back into their fields, even as stores empty and the need for food assistance surges. We see export restrictions and price hikes as experts predict dramatic increases in malnutrition globally. These failures demand that we ask not only how to repair this damage, but how to fundamentally reimagine food systems.*

Are the shortages and the pain inflicted on your wallet starting to make a little more sense now? Stimulus-response; we make the problem, we provide the solution. Funny how that works.

Scherr and Farley also inform that:

---

[89] Schwab and Malleret, *COVID-19: The Great Reset*, 2.1.1. "Acceleration of Digitization."

In 2021, the global community will develop a new action framework for the UN Convention on Biological Diversity, advance action under the UN Framework Convention on Climate Change, and begin the UN Decade for Ecosystem Restoration. Sustainable food systems must be central to these strategies.

The Food Systems Summit of 2021, called for by the UN Secretary-General, is based on the UN's premise that, "our food systems must change to achieve the goals of the 2030 Agenda." You know, living in a pod, eating bugs, and all that. As Danish Parliamentarian Ida Auken writes for the World Economic Forum in "This is what 2030 could look like if we win the war on climate change" (and notice how we're always fighting abstractions like terror and extremism, or non-physical "enemies" like viruses and climate change):

By 2030, your CO2 emissions will be greatly reduced. Meat on your dinner table will be a rare sight. . . . If you choose to call a car, an algorithm will calculate the smartest route for the vehicle. . . . Air traffic has started to decline. . . . People are trying out new types of living arrangements with more shared functions and spaces.

Already we see examples such as Portland, Oregon's Residential Infill Project, which follows in the footsteps of Vancouver, Minneapolis, and Seattle with duplex and triplex re-legalization, and Austin, Texas's "sixplex-with-affordability." There are also size limits on one-unit buildings, and four homes can be built on most residential lots. There will also, of course, be a diversity component, although the ruling class always speaks in euphemisms; writing for the Sightline Institute, Michael Andersen reports that:

Portland's new rules will also offer a 'deeper affordability' option: four to six homes on any lot if at least half are available to low-income Portlanders at regulated, affordable prices. The measure will make it viable for nonprofits to intersperse below-market housing anywhere in the city for the first time in a century.

Non-profits like the Open Society Foundation and their ilk presumably. Open Philanthropy has provided significant grant money to the Sightline

Institute; Open Philanthropy's main funders are the Jewish Facebook co-founder Dustin Moskovitz and his wife Cari Tuna.

The above-mentioned EcoAgriculture Partners, based out of Fairfax, Virginia, via their website:

> [B]rings together women's groups, farmer cooperatives, civil society organizations, universities, international NGOs, United Nations agencies, governments, and more to advance multi-stakeholder management processes in landscapes, strengthen governance strategies, and promote cross-sector research. We connect landscape leaders across national boundaries to share experiences and inspire innovations in integrated landscape management.

In case you were wondering, some of their major partners include: the Rockefeller Foundation, the World Wildlife Fund, the World Bank Group, the UNDP, the Ford Foundation, the Gates Foundation, and the US Department of Agriculture. Interesting to see the USDA and the Gates Foundation there, especially as Bill Gates is now the largest private owner of farmland in the United States. What was it Henry Kissinger said? Oh yes: "Control oil and you control nations; control food and you control the people."

Particularly germane in this context and especially as prelude to the measures imposed to ostensibly combat coronavirus—plus the UN's Agenda 2030 Sustainable Development Goals and the World Economic Forum's Great Reset "green" hogwash—is the research of one John B. Calhoun. Calhoun, it should be noted, worked on the Rodent Ecology Project at none other than Johns Hopkins University, that incubator of transgenderism and a vital institution in the genesis of the COVID-19-related tyrannies (More fun from the Johns Hopkins Center for Health Security and Department of Environmental Health and Engineering; Johns Hopkins Bloomberg School of Public Health includes five researchers in conjunction with one each from the Columbia University Mailman School of Public Health and the Department of Anthropology at Texas State University on "The SPARS Pandemic 2025–2028: A Futuristic Scenario to Facilitate Medical Countermeasure Communication," published in the University of Central Florida's *Journal of International Crisis and Risk Communication Research*), among many other extremely critical aspects of the ruling class's agenda. Calhoun also spent a year at the Stanford University Center for Advanced Study in the Behavioral Sciences.

In a nutshell, Calhoun's research essentially showed what would happen to a mouse population if all of its needs except one were provided for. This lack of one critical ingredient—space—had catastrophic consequences; in his most famous experiment begun in July 1968 under the auspices of the National Institute of Mental Health, the "mouse universe" had all of the population's needs provided for and a lack of natural predators. Soon, the mouse population began exploding exponentially, but eventually the population growth slowed down and peaked before a precipitous decline, a decline that was preceded by an extended period of social breakdown and a proliferation of aberrant behaviors including the abandonment of their young by mothers and the attacking and abuse of their offspring, odd outbursts of aggression often of a predatory nature coupled with a lack of will by many males to defend their territory, self-isolation defined by psychological withdrawal, and deviant sexuality.

With all of their needs met, the rodents never learned resource-procurement and survival skills, instead turning to what Ted Kaczynski would define as surrogate activities, mostly those pertaining to self-gratification and extensive (excessive) self-grooming. These "beautiful ones" stopped reproducing, and eventually the utopia turned dystopic, corpses clogging the living quarters and the demise of the population despite there still remaining an abundance of resources and, indeed, more space.

Today, the global human population is still exploding in much of the Third World, particularly sub-Saharan Africa, artificially subsidized by Western "elites," while the populations in the Occident and to a lesser extent the Orient are maintained by immigration of outsiders—which we are told we "need." Although the lies are increasingly wearing thin, the rhetoric generally revolves around compassion and the acceptance of refugees from conflict and "climate change" refugees. All birth rates in the First World with the exception of Israel are now below replacement-level.

It is the *perception* of over-crowding, however, that leads to humans' crowding in vast metropoles and the resultant deviant and destructive behaviors that inevitably proliferate. This is the legacy of neo-liberalism as we embark on this new era of social and biological engineering. We are not (yet?) witnessing city streets clogged with corpses, but certainly the desire to propagate and live meaningful lives has collapsed. "Social distancing" measures do not undermine the phenomenon, but rather exacerbate the total alienation needed to break down the population completely and mold them into new shapes. This is obviously by design, as the "elites" not only understand this research but have actively funded it themselves. Their restriction of food and ability to cause maximal pain in order to leverage this into the next stage of their plan is in lock-step with the efforts to create hive-like cities with their pods and bug burgers as ostensibly combatting climate change. There remains plenty of space and resources on our planet provided there is proper management and stewardship, but some real factors—drought and poor yields—have conjoined with intentional mismanagement and an artificial scarcity that has gripped the globe, with crops being left to rot in fields and an intentional move to all things "green" in the global Green New Deal/Great Reset/Agenda 2030 in tandem with COVID-19 lockdowns and other gross over-extensions by the powerful. Labor issues that dovetail neatly with coronavirus restrictions and mandates are another major factor. It is both manipulation and coercion on multiple fronts in order to produce the desired result.

The "elites" have turned the entire globe into one of Calhoun's rodent universes, and we are now living in a downward trajectory as top-down measures are implemented to maneuver the collapsed and demoralized populations into their new post-human existence, a new world where they reign not just like gods but as God. As Calhoun wrote in "Death Squared: The Explosive Growth and Demise of a Mouse Population":

> *I shall largely speak of mice, but my thoughts are on man, on healing, on life and its evolution. Threatening life and evolution are the two deaths, death of the spirit and death of the body. Evolution, in terms of ancient wisdom, is the acquisition of access to the tree of life. This takes us back to the white first horse of the Apocalypse which with its rider set out to conquer the forces that threaten the spirit with death. Further in Revelation (ii.7) we note: 'To him who conquers I will grant to eat the tree of life, which is in the paradise of God' and further on (Rev. xxii.2): 'The leaves of the tree were for the healing of nations.' This takes us to the fourth horse of the Apocalypse (Rev. vi.7): 'I saw . . . a pale horse, and its rider's name was Death, and Hades followed him; and they were given power over a fourth of the earth, to kill with the sword and with famine and with pestilence and by wild beasts of the earth. . . .' This second death has gradually become the predominant concern of modern medicine. . . .*

Perhaps we might do well to reflect upon another of John's transcriptions (Rev. ii. 1): 'He who conquers shall not be hurt by the second death.'

As we have seen in the words and deeds of the transhumanists, they want to live forever. This passage as clear as any other evinces the true nature of this project. Though science and medicine are now oriented in finding the keys to eternal life and youth, the first death—death of the spirit—is actively encouraged. It is the only way we turn our eyes from eternity beyond this world and root ourselves totally in this one. To quote Hunter S. Thompson, it isn't "a whole subculture of frightened illiterates with no faith in anything," but a whole culture period, with Progress and Science as inextricable and the one saving grace, the one lifeline of faith in the morass of meaninglessness. We are instructed to put our faith in the high priests in lab coats, who will deliver the magic elixir or possibly the global kill-shot for the unworthy.

Whether it's a weeding-out, a harvesting of the quantum computing power of the human brain and the using of our bodies and minds as nodes in the Internet of All Things, and/or using the population as guinea pigs for the "real deal," this ceaseless desire for "upgrading" humanity has been a major preoccupation of at least one faction of the "elites" for quite some time; as Whitney Webb and Jeremy Loffredo report for *Unlimited Hangout*: "One particular Operation Warp Speed vaccine . . . has not only had a host of safety issues but was also developed by researchers with deep ties to the British Eugenics Society, which changed its name in 1989 to the Galton Institute." It changed its name once again in 2021 to the Adelphi Genetics Forum. The transhumanist Julian Huxley was a President of the British Eugenics Society (1959–1962). Arthur Balfour, of the infamous Balfour Declaration, was also a member. There are deep ties between the Galton Institute, the Wellcome Trust ("Climate change is a global health problem already impacting millions of people around the world"), and the developers of the Oxford-AstraZeneca COVID-19 "vaccine." So the desire to "upgrade" humanity via eugenics is the through-line, but it has adapted as technology has developed and medicine has advanced. It has also become more ideological and abstract.

The American counterpart of the British Eugenics Society/Galton Institute/ Adelphi Genetics Forum, which is now called the Society for Biodemography and Social Biology, is currently helmed by Hans-Peter Kohler;

his University of Pennsylvania biographical description, where he is the Frederick J. Warren Professor of Demography, Professor of Sociology, and Co-Director of the Population Aging Research Center, states:

> *Hans-Peter Kohler's primary research focuses on fertility and health in developing and developed countries. A key characteristic of this research is the attempt to integrate demographic, economic, socio-logical and biological approaches in empirical and theoretical mod-els of demographic behavior. For example, Kohler has been investi-gating the bio-social determinants of fertility . . . the importance of social interaction processes for fertility and AIDS-related behaviors, and demographic methods for measuring and forecasting fertility trends.*

One of the co-founders of the American Eugenics Society and a British Eu-genics Society member to boot, Frederick Osborn, concluded that their particular vision would have to take place under a different name because eugenics is routinely seen as "Nazi" by the left.

Why Jews and other "elites" would subscribe to something so contrary to the narrative that's been shaped since World War II surrounding eugen-ics lies in the very simple fact that these constructed narratives are just that: constructs. In reality, Jews have long "borrowed" from the genes of Europeans especially, and have also emphasized certain breeding charac-teristics within the "in-group" to produce particular outcomes. The latter is often rigidly policed; as John Glad outlines in his 2011 book *Jewish Eugen-ics*, traditional Jewish culture has long been eugenic in nature, and, indeed, Zionism itself was conceived as a grand eugenic plan. For Glad:

> *["Father of Zionism" Theodore] Herzl's partner in Zionism, the pop-ular eugenicist Max Nordau, saw Herzl's proposal as straightfor-ward eugenics: the then popular Lamarckian belief in the heritabil-ity of acquired characteristics lent hope that the scrawny, weak, and inferior Jew – an image internalized by many Jews – would become physically strong, sexually potent, and morally fit. Envisaged as re-placing both the ghetto Jews and the "effete" coffee house Jews, this image was subsequently transmogrified into that of Zionist "fighting Jews" who established the Jewish state by force of arms. Created by Ephraim Moses Lilien, the "first Zionist artist," the*

illustrations were intended to illustrate the ideal of Nordau's "muscle Jew."[90]

We can see in this conception of Zionism a conscious invocation of the *Übermensch*, which is considered integral to the National Socialist movement. Clearly there is an antagonism here, and it is not coincidental that the Vienna of Hitler is also the Vienna of Herzl. That said, as Glad argues:

> *Given the massive assault on the eugenics movement as a supposedly 'anti-Semitic' ideology of genocide, however, historical veracity requires that the distorted image produced over the last four decades be rectified. The topic is not merely an important fragment in the rich and vibrant mosaic of Jewish intellectual history. Far more important, it will determine the survival of culture itself. . . . This misapprehension stands in gross contradiction to the grand tradition of Jewish culture and is the product of diligent propaganda manufactured by a heavily Jewish group.*[91]

This through-line of eugenics in the Jewish culture here intersects with their pole position in society and the ideology/religion of transhumanism. As a consequence, we will also see Gentiles involved and, indeed, integral. The transhumanist project is itself eugenic in the sense that one of the major strains aims to create actual superhumans, with the other aiming to create a superbeing totally beyond humanity. In either case, like transgenderism, in order to be fully grasped, transhumanism must be understood in the context of its "Jewishness."

Returning to Frederick Osborn, he ended up becoming the president of the Population Council, succeeding founder and eugenics enthusiast John D. Rockefeller III. The Population Council is still active; it is funded by a host of establishment organizations: the UK's DFID, USAID, the CDC, the NIH, Zambia's National HIV/AIDS/STI/TB Council, the World Bank Group, the World Health Organization, several UN branches, the University of California-San Francisco, the Sackler Institute for Nutrition Science (yes, those Sacklers), Stanford University, the American Jewish World Service, the London School of Economics and Political Science, the

---

[90] Glad, Jewish Eugenics, 6.
[91] Ibid., 9–10.

International Planned Parenthood Federation, the Harvard T.H. Chan School of Public Health, the UK's ODI, Johns Hopkins University, the Tides Foundation, the MacArthur Foundation, the WK Kellogg Foundation, the Microsoft Matching Gifts Program, the AmazonSmile Foundation, the Ford Foundation, the Gates Foundation, Pfizer Workplace Giving, and the Aga Khan Foundation, among others.

Showing the interconnectedness of the global system, Aga Khan Foundation, affiliated with the Population Council, is in turn, for example, partnered with a wide range of organizations and governments, such as: the Government of New Zealand, the Government of Japan, Microsoft, the Government of India, the Unilever Foundation, Johnson & Johnson, BNP Paribas, the Government of Egypt, Global Affairs Canada, the European Commission and the European Union, Cargill, the Mastercard Foundation, the African Development Bank, UN Food and Agriculture, the World Bank, the International Atomic Energy Agency, the UN World Food Programme, the UN High Commissioner for Refugees, the World Health Organization, the EPA, USAID, the US State Department, the Smithsonian Institution, the US Department of Agriculture, the MacArthur Foundation, Harvard University, the Ford Foundation, the Gates Foundation, MIT, Johns Hopkins University, and the Rockefeller Foundation.

Returning to the motives of men like Rockefeller and Osborn, they clearly understood that overpopulation hysteria would certainly sell better than forceful sterilization, and eugenics had become a dirty word after World War II. As an interesting side note, Pfizer and BioNTech finalized the Phase 2/3 study protocol of their COVID-19 "vaccine" in response to feedback from global regulators, including the FDA and the German Paul-Ehrlich-Institut. Though this institute is not named for the same Paul Ehrlich, it is an intriguing coincidence (if you want to call it that) that the Jewish Paul Ehrlich, author of the 1968 book *The Population Bomb* and Bing Professor Emeritus of Population Studies of the Department of Biology of Stanford University and President of Stanford's Center for Conservation Biology, is one of the primary popularizers of the over-population hysteria coinciding with the first significant public concerns about climate change. Ehrlich actually mentioned global warming from greenhouse gases as an antidote to the feared cooling effect of aerosols in 1968. Uh oh!

The Rockefeller Foundation was, along with the Ford Foundation, integral—and continues to be integral—to the engineered globalist vision, including the "Green Revolution" that contributed to the population boom in the first place and pushed so many small-scale agrarian farmers off their farms and into the factories and cities, replete with mass use of pesticides, pollutants, and bio-engineered (genetically-modified/GMO) crops. Though over-population remains an occasionally-voiced concern, its morphing into general climate hysteria in the latter third of the twentieth century has certainly borne fruit as justification for a variety of measures associated with the present agenda. The Rockefeller Foundation has made climate change one of their central issues, and note not just the usual buzzwords but also the ubiquitous yet ill-defined connection to the pandemic in the following from their press release "New Blueprint Provides Opportunities to Leverage Trillions of Dollars of Global Institutional Investors to Combat Climate Change":

> *Mike Muldoon, Managing Director of Innovative Finance at The Rockefeller Foundation added, "The private sector is needed now more than ever to tackle the growing divergence between the developed world where vaccines and economic stimulus are bountiful, and the developing world where they are not. . . . These recommendations provide a clear path towards increased private sector mobilization as we collectively seek to respond to the pandemic and drive a green and equitable recovery."*

What do vaccines have to do with climate change?

This is the same Rockefeller Foundation that simulated the various pandemic scenarios in their May 2010 report with the Global Business Network and now wants to sell us the pre-planned solution. In fact, they had one ready-made in 2020 with its *National COVID-19 Testing and Tracing Action Plan*, which will, naturally, expand the use of data and surveillance and which incorporates "racial equity" data as rhetoric of transhumanism becomes inextricably intertwined with that of neo-liberalism:

- *Speed integration of testing and tracing data systems.*
- *Consistently collect and act on racial equity data.*
- *Plan for the arrival of home and employer testing. We'll need these technologies to get to 30 million tests per week, but many states do not have a robust approach to integrating these results into their public health surveillance systems.*

- *Moving from descriptive analytics to predictive analytics and policy modeling.*[92]

The document also states that "human behavior will increasingly become the limiting factor in the efficacy of these systems."[93] Thus we see here hints of the transhumanist religion of Dataism where the systems themselves and especially the algorithms driving them become sovereign and humans as they once were become superfluous—should they not find themselves committed to the Singularity. Human behavior must, at minimum, becoming modified to fit the system, not the other way around. For reference, the contributors to their report included a number of individuals with the Rockefeller Foundation as well as those tied to the furtherance of this agenda, such as the University of Minnesota, Duke University, Harvard University (Harvard Global Health Institute, etc.), the University of Pennsylvania, the University of Chicago, and Johns Hopkins (Raymond Pearl of Johns Hopkins University was the first president of the International Union for the Scientific Study of Population, formed in 1927), plus Deloitte, the American Enterprise Institute, and the Scripps Translational Research Institute (in 1922, the Scripps Foundation for Research in Population Problems was founded in 1922; it would later be renamed the Scripps Gerontology Center in 1972).

Also sitting at the intersection of medical tyranny and big data/technology is the World Health Organization. You may recognize them from the ongoing COVID-19 saga as a preeminent authority on all things coronavirus. In addition to the centrality of data as they readily acknowledge, per their Immunization Agenda 2030:

> *The COVID-19 pandemic has reminded the world of the power of vaccines. . . . Immunization is playing a critical role in achieving the [United Nations] Sustainable Development Goals (SDGs). Immunization reaches more people than any other health and social service, making it the foundation of primary health care systems and a key driver toward universal health coverage. This makes immunization critical to SDG3. . . . Because health is so fundamental to development, IA2030 will also contribute—either directly or indirectly—*

---

[92] Rockefeller Foundation, *National COVID-19*, 45.
[93] Ibid.

to 13 of the other SDGs. Immunization is an investment for the fu-
ture, creating a healthier, safer and more prosperous world for all.

Also of significance is the fact that WHO Director-General Tedros Ad-
hanom Ghebreyesus's Chief Advisor Senait Fisseha was appointed as the
director of International Programs at the Susan Thompson Buffett Foundation, described by Influence Watch as having been "founded in 1964 by
investor Warren Buffett, reportedly to address Buffett's 'Malthusian dread'
of population growth among the global poor." Its president is Buffett's
daughter's ex-husband Allen Greenberg, a former legal aide to Chuck
Schumer. The organization has donated millions of dollars to the World
Health Organization and John D. Rockefeller III's Population Council, a
partner with the Ford Foundation (a major donor itself to the Population
Council) and the International Planned Parenthood Federation (IPPF), per
Influence Watch, "on large-scale IUD programs throughout the 1960s in
India, Pakistan, South Korea, and Taiwan." Additionally, Buffett an-
nounced in 2006 a "philanthropic merger" with the Gates Foundation. As
Joseph D'Agostino writes for *Population Research Institute*:

> *Gates has put his money where his mouth is. His foundation gave*
> *$2.25 million to Johns Hopkins to train Third World experts in pop-*
> *ulation control in 1997. In 1998, his foundation–which is controlled*
> *by Gates, his wife, and his father–gave $1.7 million to a United Na-*
> *tions Population Fund program for controlling population growth.*
> *Buffett has given millions to pro-abortion and population control*
> *efforts over the years. . . . How much of a priority is it for him? Re-*
> *ported the Chronicle of Philanthropy, Nov. 13, 1997, about his wife's*
> *foundation, "One of the foundation's directors, Mr. Buffett's daugh-*
> *ter, Susie, told* The Chronicle *that she did expect that population*
> *control would be the foundation's top priority. 'That's what my fa-*
> *ther has always believed was the biggest and most important issue,*
> *so that will be the focus,' she said. 'I feel as his child that it's im-*
> *portant to carry out his wishes. It's his money.'"*

Some familiar names and faces there, eh? In this push for their vision of
sustainability, clearly select areas (animal husbandry stands out) and populations (European stock and their artificially-suppressed birth rates
stands out) have been selected for strategic downsizing. Other population

groups, particularly those of the Third World, have been used as test subjects by various entities for a very long time. What's clear is that at this point, they're not letting anyone off this ride, even if it takes most of us right off a cliff.

Chapter Six:
Make the Money, Break the Money,
Make the Money

"We don't have enough money to get home, we don't have enough money to eat, we don't have enough money to sleep!"   – Harry Dunne

What do you get the guy who has everything? A brand-new currency, that's what! Digital, if you please. Smart.

According to Extended Monaco, the Monaco Digital Advisory Council places:

> [A]n emphasis on the importance of formulating a detailed action plan, building a strong brand (now Extended Monaco) and developing a Monegasque smart city, based on the Internet of Things as well as a 100% digital administration. Connecting people, vehicles and infrastructure, promoting soft mobility, developing a platform using Blockchain technology. . . . The first pivotal moment was in summer 2019, when the Principality became the first country in the world to roll out 5G across its entire territory, in partnership with Huawei. This roll-out represents an important driver of growth for many sectors of the economy (the smart city, media, transport, e-health) and a font of opportunities, including the use of smart drones by firefighters, the development of self-driving vehicles, telemedicine, and so on. Like 4G before it, 5G will open up a new range of possibilities that are as yet difficult to qualify and quantify.

So something like that, where the currency is blockchain-based and thus every step, every transaction can be traced, everything can be inextricably intertwined. Fully digitized, in implication it would ultimately require no human oversight, placing you at the mercy of algorithms and artificial intelligence. In essence, it could run of its own volition, with the only human inputs being those where people have been merged with the system in some capacity.

Think about it like this: the stock market is already mostly an AI playground; in the same way that by some estimations almost half of social media is populated by bots, estimates are that automatic trading systems account for 70 to 80 percent or more of shares traded on US stock exchanges. This, of course, benefits those who have already accrued massive wealth, as advancements in AI greatly increases the capacity at which these individuals—or more accurately their algorithms—are able to trade. High-Frequency Trading (HFT) is one example where those with the means and access create algorithms to monitor the market and rapidly buy and sell faster than humanly possible. There is no equal access for the individual trader; consequently, a disproportionate amount of power is given to those with the resources and ability to operate HFT systems. In a financialized economy and, indeed, society, this exacerbates the wealth gap to such a degree that it becomes radically imbalanced. It also concentrates yet more power into the hands of the few who can continuously game the system to their benefit. The Occupy Wall Street movement understood this, which is why the power players began pushing niche "social causes" and reviving racial grievances in order to distract people from what could've been a legitimately society-altering left-right coalition. If you're screaming about the oxymoron known as gay marriage, you're not as focused on BlackRock outbidding you by $30,000 for a house so you stay stuck in a crappy apartment that costs more than the mortgage would've. See how this works?

We all know that the currency in circulation—so much so that it's triggered massive inflation way outpacing wage increases, and this is almost certainly by design, but we'll come back to this—is not tethered to anything tangible. But let's underscore how completely abstract the whole financial system truly is. On May 6th, 2010, for around a half an hour in the afternoon, approximately *one trillion dollars* in market value was lost, and all based on the fact that a large, automated selling program was rapidly executed in the E-mini S&P 500 stock index futures market; blamed on the

Greek debt crisis, it was more so that of an algorithmic avalanche, with over two billion shares traded by algorithms in less than twenty minutes at one point. HFT systems can flood markets with orders that are canceled in microseconds, faster than any human can respond, and make the market that much more volatile. This was over a decade ago, and given Moore's law, imagine how much more prominent this technology has become, to the point where the market is basically its own system irrespective of genuine interpersonal interaction/commerce. We react to it, rather than the other way around, in so many cases.

The International Organization of Securities Commissions (IOSCO) Technical Committee published its *Regulatory Issues Raised by the Impact of Technological Changes on Market Integrity and Efficiency: Consultation Report* in July 2011, where it noted that:

> *At its most complex, [algorithmic trading] may entail many algorithms that are able to assimilate information from multiple markets in different assets and to use this to implement a high-speed, multi-asset trading strategy that transacts numerous inter-related trades in fractions of a second. For instance, algorithms may now be designed to predict the presence and actions of other algorithms, thereby attempting to stay one step ahead of them. . . .*
>
> *The use of* dark liquidity *for the trading of equities and the development of so-called dark pools and dark orders has increased. . . .*
>
> *Dark liquidity has long existed, for example, in the form of orders being held by* upstairs trading *desks and liquidity offered by firms that internalise their order flow. What is new is the degree of automation of trading in dark pools and dark orders on equity trading venues, and the widespread availability of their use. . . .*
>
> *Market fragmentation and the presence of dark liquidity may raise concerns around transparency.*[94]

In short, as Investopedia puts it, "these trades are concealed from the public until after they are executed; these transactions are obscure like dark, murky water." For Will Kenton, writing for Investopedia:

---

[94] IOSCO Technical Committee, *Regulatory Issues Raised*, 10, 13–4.

> *HFT is a method of trading that uses powerful computer programs to transact a large number of orders in fractions of a second; in general, traders with the fastest execution speeds are more profitable than traders with slower execution speeds.*
>
> *With HFT, institutional traders can execute their massive orders—oftentimes multimillion-share blocks—ahead of other investors, allowing them to capitalize on fractional upticks or downticks in share prices. As soon as subsequent orders are executed, HFT traders can close out their positions and almost instantly obtain profits. This can occur dozens of times a day and can result in huge gains for HFT traders.*

Mirroring the neo-feudal two-tiered society in the process of being created, the advent of the two-tiered market sees certain firms pay extra for the ability to access data and servers which provide their traders a significant advantage over the plebs. "These are the leads, and you don't get them," as it were. In fact, many firms leverage their financial means and influence to gain access to information that would not be available to the average investor, and then buy and sell stocks based on that info, employing their HFT systems and outpacing human performance. This is called front-running, and it's done a lot.

Keeping with the theme of dark, shadowy mechanisms employed by the dark, shadowy financiers and their machines (the reader may notice the sheer volume of allusions to the ghost in the machine and various other dark occultic symbols and symbolism), high frequency trading may also be responsible for a phenomenon known as phantom liquidity, which is when HFTs place and then almost instantaneously cancel massive numbers of trade orders to create the illusion of either greater supply or demand for a stock to advantageously manipulate price. Machine learning can also distill information and execute trades in a pulse-like manner, which creates much more volatility. The volatility is capitalized upon by these very same algorithms that are working at literally inhuman speeds. Yes, the humans who are positioned to do so will continue to capitalize ever more dramatically, but we may well already be at our black box moment with AI and the stock market as it becomes a closed system divorced from humans unless, again, they find a way to merge with the system.

Far-fetched? Since at least 1998, the technology has been available for certain implants that can be used as part of the Internet of All Things, when

Professor Kevin Warwick, director of cybernetics at the University of Reading, had a microchip implanted in his arm. In 2005, "biohacker" Amal Graafstra had a radio-frequency identification (RFID) transponder implanted into his left hand. In 2014, Bitcoin entrepreneur Martin Wismeijer had a near-field communications (NFC) chip implanted into his hand; the chip is the same type of technology built into the Apple Pay digital payment system and found in many Android devices, enabling, as Eliene Augenbraun writes, "devices to send data back and forth, enabling the user to make mobile payments or send commands to other smart devices... The chip...is similar to what Americans are beginning to see embedded into their credit cards and mobile phones, including the Apple iPhone 6." Wismeijer did this because he "wanted to experiment with storing Bitcoins using subdermal implants." UK firm BioTeq has been making implanted, "contactless" chips since 2017. With the explosion in Bitcoin and other cryptocurrencies, as well as the push for central bank digital currencies (CBDCs), we would do well to keep this aspect in mind, especially as everything from let's call it medical status (such as a "vaccine") and social credit can and will eventually be tied into this implantable currency. Without it, one may not buy or sell; or should one find themselves in poor standing, the same.

Already in 2019, MIT researchers announced that they had created an embeddable ink that would be injected along with a vaccine and visible using a smartphone app and filter. The research into this quantum dot tattoo—specifically geared toward children in the promotional press releases—was funded in large part by the Bill and Melinda Gates Foundation, which in 2010 at the World Economic Forum's Annual Meeting called for a "decade of vaccines." Yissum, the Technology Transfer Company of the Hebrew University of Jerusalem and licenser of an extensive quantum dot technology patent portfolio to Nanosys, has partnered with companies such as Google, Johnson & Johnson, Merck, Microsoft, and Novartis. Hebrew University also announced in December 2019 that it had "reinvented the concept of the periodic table but for artificial atoms." Nanosys has hundreds of patents related to quantum dot construction and component and manufacturing design. This quantum dot technology will almost certainly form an integral part of the future vaccination identification program—a "green card" for personal carbon credits or purely digitized finances tied to biometric data.

In 2018, ID2020 Alliance Partners, working in partnership with the United Nations High Commissioner for Refugees (UNHCR), drafted a "formal articulation of our perspective on ethical approaches to digital identity," which includes in its Manifesto the statement that "The ability to prove one's identity is a fundamental and universal human right," and that "For some, including refugees, the stateless, and other marginalized groups [who often discard their identity cards before illegally entering Western countries so they won't be deported], reliance on national identification systems isn't possible," once again creating another globalized, trans/supra-national alternative. ID2020, according to its website, "is coordinating funding for identity and channeling those funds toward high-impact projects, enabling diverse stakeholders—UN agencies, NGOs, governments, and enterprises—to pursue a coordinated approach that creates a pathway for efficient and responsible implementation at scale." In addition to Mastercard, some of its other partners include Microsoft, Accenture, GAVI ("The Vaccine Alliance"), the Rockefeller Foundation, and iRespond.

iRespond, another NGO "dedicated to using biometrics to improve lives through digital identity," in turn also partners with organizations such as the World Health Organization, the Johns Hopkins Bloomberg School of Public Health, the IOM, the International Rescue Committee (IRC), and the CDC. Whitney Webb for *Unlimited Hangout* notes:

> *iRespond . . . has begun piloting a new biometric program for newborns among the predominately Karen refugee population along the Myanmar-Thailand border, a program it soon hopes to "quickly deploy" at a greater scale and make available to the general global population. The pilot program is being conducted as part of the controversial ID2020 alliance. . . .*
>
> *The pilot program is being conducted at the Mae Tao clinic, which is largely funded by the CIA cut-out USAID as well as the governments of Germany and Taiwan, the Open Society Foundations and the International Rescue Committee (IRC). . . .*
>
> *Having a "digital identity" would allow refugees "to access improved, consistent healthcare within the camp" with plans for the same system to eventually "electronically document both educational attainment and professional skills to aid with employment opportunities. . . ."*

This program is remarkably similar to the World Food Pro-gramme's recently implemented "Building Blocks" initiative, which is funded by the US, German, Dutch and Luxembourgian govern-ments. . . .

iRespond's system, not unlike Trust Stamp's, is also slated to serve as a vaccine record.

Interesting to see this connected to food, but as I've evidenced, the One World/New World Order system wants to bring everything under its con-trol through these linkages, and then to "plug in" everything from there.

It is not surprising to see Taiwan involved when in July 2022 Taiwan announced that its digital COVID vaccine certificate would be com-patible with the SMART Health Card (also issued by many US states, Canadian provinces, the city of Sydney in Australia, companies like Walmart and CVS, hundreds of healthcare facilities, and other na-tional governments such as those of Senegal and Japan). Taiwan is also part of the EU Digital COVID Certificate (EU-DCC) program and the Vaccination Credential Initiative (VCI), which per its website is "a voluntary coalition of public and private organizations committed to empowering individuals access to a trustworthy and verifiable copy of their vaccination records in digital or paper form using open, interoperable standards. . . . VCI [leads] the development and imple-mentation of the open-source SMART Health Card Framework and specifications." VCI members include Amazon, Apple, Blockchain Labs, a bunch of universities, Google, the Government of Aruba, the Province of Ontario Ministry of Health, the States of California and New York, Microsoft, iCrypto, Technical Writers of India, the Mayo Clinic, the Energy Alliance Group of North America ("helps identify and provide green energy solutions for businesses, residential build-ings, and more"), V-Health Passport, the Commons Project (which was established with the help of the Rockefeller Foundation; Execu-tive Founder and President Paul Meyer's resume includes the Coun-cil on Foreign Relations, the Aspen Institute, International Rescue Committee, and the 1992 Clinton campaign, and he was a Young Global Leader with the World Economic Forum), and the Parker Jew-ish Institute.

Returning to the aforementioned Trust Stamp, according to its web-site, it "is an artificial intelligence company that primarily develops proprietary identity solutions to help determine whether an individual is who they say they are and that they can be trusted, including Trust Stamp's AI-powered facial biometrics." Their Advisory Board includes individuals such as: James Gaughran (Department of Defense; a Special Agent with the US Secret Service; Deputy Assistant Inspector General at the Department of Homeland Security), Sarah-Jill Lennard (a former UK Diplomat and former Chief Security Officer & Chief Information Security Officer for Deloitte), Buffy Christie (JPMorgan Chase), and Sam Guttman (formerly served as Inspector in Charge with the US Postal Inspection Service where he led the agency's first initiatives to use forensic computer analysis of data in investigative work).

The Trust Stamp system is a prototype for dispensing with cash altogether and the uniting of all types of credit (including social) in one digital format; as Raul Diego reports for *Mint Press News*:

> A biometric digital identity platform that "evolves just as you evolve" is set to be introduced in "low-income, remote communities" in West Africa thanks to a public-private partnership between the Bill Gates-backed GAVI vaccine alliance, Mastercard and the AI-powered "identity authentication" company, Trust Stamp.
>
> The program, which was first launched in late 2018, will see Trust Stamp's digital identity platform integrated into the GAVI-Mastercard "Wellness Pass," a digital vaccination record and identity system that is also linked to Mastercard's click-to-play system that powered by its AI and machine learning technology called NuData. Mastercard, in addition to professing its commitment to promoting "centralized record keeping of childhood immunization" also describes itself as a leader toward a "World Beyond Cash," and its partnership with GAVI marks a novel approach towards linking a biometric digital identity system, vaccination records, and a payment system into a single cohesive platform. The effort, since its launch nearly two years ago, has been funded via $3.8 million in GAVI donor funds in addition to a matched donation of the same amount by the Bill and Melinda Gates Foundation. . . .
>
> Mastercard announced that Trust Stamp's biometric identity platform would be integrated into Wellness Pass as Trust Stamp's system is capable of providing biometric identity in areas of the world lacking internet access or cellular connectivity and also does

not require knowledge of an individual's legal name or identity to function. The Wellness Program . . . will be coupled with a COVID-19 vaccination program.

There are state efforts along these lines (such as in Lithuania, where they've restricted "non-essential services" to only those who possess the grotesquely-named Freedom ID) and supra-state efforts such as the European Union's Digital COVID Certificate. Meanwhile the media was denigrating legitimate treatments such as ivermectin in favor of lowering testosterone in men or using antidepressants as a treatment for the virus. This is where we are now, and again we can see the synchronization of the many issues confronting our society being brought into neat alignment but in an inverse relationship with reality. Now it is true that the omicron variant seemed to infect men to a greater degree, but should we continue to tank what's left of our collective testosterone and in the process wreck our immune systems further? Of course not, but a sick, scared, and dumb population is much more compliant and easily-manipulated.

With the apparent *need* for a global final solution to the human problem, according to the World Economic Forum (WEF), "With countries experiencing unprecedented challenges and impact under the COVID-19 pandemic, the Forum has launched the COVID Action Platform in collaboration with the World Health Organization (WHO)" to further their agenda by using the man-made COVID-19 to continue to turn the world into a giant laboratory. Some of the platform projects include (with descriptions from the WEF website):

- *COVID-19 Financial Services Response Network: Project by the International Monetary Fund (IMF)*
- *Pandemic Supply Chain Network (PSCN): Engagement from the International Organization for Migration (IOM), United Nations Children's Fund (UNICEF), World Bank Group, and World Health Organization (WHO)*
- *Managing Epidemics with Consumer Wearables (helmed by the WEF): Policymakers from Estonia and Rwanda as well as the World Health Organization (WHO) have participated in the project community and provided regular input via interviews and workshop participation, along with private companies such as Amazon Web Services, Apple, Facebook, IBM and Xiaomi.*

- *The Epidemic Big Data Resource and Analytics Innovation Net-work (helmed by the WHO): (EPI-BRAIN) is an innovative global platform that allows experts in data and public health to analyze large data-sets for emergency preparedness and re-sponse. Through big data and artificial intelligence, the network aims to improve the prediction towards the outbreak as well as strengthen the response to the pandemic. Currently, the Minis-try of Health from Bangladesh, Finland, Germany, Singapore and the United States, and the International Air Transport As-sociation have joined the project community together with . . . private organizations to reduce the impact of outbreaks through forecasting and predictive analytics.*

Partner organizations for EPI-BRAIN include the Gates Foundation, GAVI ("The Vaccine Alliance"), the World Bank, Harvard University, the United Nations Foundation, the US HHS, USAID, Novo Nordisk, the Nigerian CDC, Nielsen, the Korean CDC, Médecins Sans Frontières, Johnson & John-son, PATH, and CEPI.

In late 2020, Turkey announced the launch of its Centre for the Fourth Industrial Revolution Network, becoming the latest member of the Centre for the Fourth Industrial Revolution (C4IR) Network of the World Eco-nomic Forum (WEF). With centers in thirteen countries, "the Centre for the Fourth Industrial Revolution Network works with governments, lead-ing companies, civil society, innovators and experts from around the world to pilot new approaches to technology adoption and governance." Found-ing partners of this network include Palantir, Salesforce, Facebook, Huawei, IBM, Visa, Microsoft, Mitsubishi Chemical, the Inter-American Development Bank, Saudi Aramco, the Bahrain Economic Development Board, Takeda, Netflix, Splunk: The Data-to-Everything Platform Built for the Cloud, Cyberdyne, and GAVI—the Vaccine Alliance (whose founding partners are the World Health Organization, the World Bank, the Gates Foundation, and UNICEF). GAVI's major funders include Mastercard, the Rockefeller Foundation, the Coca-Cola Foundation, the Government of China, the European Commission, the US Government, the Kingdom of Saudi Arabia, the Visa Foundation, TikTok, Unilever, the International Federation of Pharmaceutical Wholesalers, the Government of Australia, the Government of Canada, UPS, Salesforce, Google, and more.

The World Economic Forum is indicative of the general thrust of this globalist-transhumanist agenda, addressing the totality of its world-shaping project with its all-encompassing Great Reset. Connecting to the various strands of globalism feeding into the rotten center, the WEF's myriad Global Future Councils include those on: Media, Entertainment, and Culture (featuring representatives of ADDO AI, the Media Development Investment Fund, and McKinsey); Cybersecurity (featuring representatives of Human Rights Watch, Credit Suisse, S&P Global, the Netherlands Cyber Security Council, PayPal, the Chinese Academy of Social Sciences, and the Cyber Security Programme at the Organization of American States); and Digital Economy and New Value Creation ("Themes include digital stewardship, shaping new value pools and emergent industries, rethinking business models and business fundamentals, building new ecosystems, creating sustainable value from data, investing for digital inclusion and assessing the disruptive impact of new technologies such as 5G and AI.... The Platform on Digital Economy and New Value Creation helps companies leverage technology to be agile in the face of disruption and to create the new digitally enabled business models for a new normal – post-COVID, purpose driven, sustainable and inclusive."). The partners for this last Platform include AstraZeneca, BlackRock, Salesforce, SWIFT, Palantir, PayPal, NBCUniversal, Lloyds Banking Group, Microsoft, Google, Grain Management, Huawei, Barclays, Bain and Company, Deutsche Bank, and more.

Other Global Future Councils include: Energy Technologies; Europe (includes Karen Donfried, President of the German Marshall Fund of the US and Mark Leonard, Director of the European Council on Foreign Relations; their website includes a mention of "contagious ideas"); Financial and Monetary Systems (includes representatives of the IMF, Facebook, Infosys, Visa, Citi, the Inter-American Development Bank, and the China National Gold Group); Geopolitics (includes representatives of the RAND Corporation, the Brookings Institution, Chatham House, the Belfer Center for Science and International Affairs-Harvard Kennedy School of Government, the International Institute for Strategic Studies, a pair of UAE government officials, the Special Representative of the Secretary-General for Iraq and Head of the United Nations Assistance Mission for Iraq, the Blavatnik School of Government-University of Oxford, and the Center for International Political Economy-Peking University); Global Public Goods in the Fourth Industrial Revolution (includes representatives of the UNDP, Mozilla, and Alphabet); Health and Healthcare (includes representatives of Lazard, Harvard Medical School, Bayer Pharmaceuticals, IBM, Kaiser Permanente); Mobility; the New Economic Agenda (features representatives of the Omidyar Network, BlackRock, Salesforce, Novartis, and the Artificial and Natural Intelligence Toulouse Institute); the New Education and Work Agenda; the New Equality and Inclusion Agenda; Space Technology (includes representatives of Airbus, Virgin Galactic, MIT, and the United Nations Office for Outer Space Affairs); and Longevity (includes representatives of the National Academy of Medicine, AARP, the Mailman School of Public Health at Columbia University, the Harvard School of Public Health, Mohammed Bin Rashid University of Medicine and Health Sciences in the United Arab Emirates, The Financial Times Group, the World Bank, and the World Health Organization).

The World Economic Forum's Global Future Council on Cities and Urbanization features representatives from the SENSEable City Laboratory at MIT, HSBC Holdings, Bloomberg Philanthropies, the Development Research Center of the State Council (DRC)-People's Republic of China, UN Habitat, the OECD, the African Development Bank (AfDB), the European Bank for Reconstruction and Development (EBRD), Housing and Urban Development of the Inter-American Development Bank, and various "global cities" like Dubai, Melbourne, New York City, and Amsterdam. Miguel Gamiño of Mastercard is also on the Council.

Mastercard has also rolled out a carbon footprint tracker; a key part of this initiative with co-developers Doconomy—"an impact-tech start up investing in new measures to help tackle climate change" in Sweden also partnered with the Finnish Ålandsbanken and the United Nations Framework Convention on Climate Change—is the Priceless Planet Coalition, which includes partners such as: Barclays, American Airlines, the Shanghai Commercial and Savings Bank, BMO Financial Group ("Inspired by the UN Sustainable Development goals and grounded in its values of integrity, empathy, diversity and responsibility"), Expo 2020 Dubai, Eurobank, Hellenic Bank, GLS Bank ("sustainability is in our DNA"), JetBlue, LL Bean, HSBC, the London Transport Museum, the PGA Tour, Major League Baseball, the MTA, Saks Fifth Avenue, and A1 Telekom Austria AG, among many others.

Mastercard is partnered with the ID2020 Digital Identity Alliance and is committed to the climate change agenda. Jo Ann Stonier, Chief Data Officer of Mastercard and a member of the World Economic Forum's Global Future Council on Consumption writes for the WEF's website that "responsible data use can accelerate a sustainable society." In a July 27, 2020 piece for the WEF website entitled "We need to talk about big data and genomics. Here's why—and how," the authors write:

> DNA (genomic data) is sometimes seen as the purest and most personal kind of data, fundamental to our identity and existence. As part of the global endeavour to understand human health and address suffering, we would be right to expect our scientists, clinicians and academic institutions to be gathering, storing, analysing, and to some extent sharing, our DNA and medical information. . . .
>
> Whilst data might be de-identified — that is, with names and addresses removed — an issue people should be aware of is that anonymity cannot be absolutely guaranteed. Health information, for instance, can always be linked to other personal information that is also available on the web – and in our increasingly data-connected world, it becomes entirely feasible that people could, in theory, be identified from their DNA alone. Do people mind? What could happen?

These are the exact questions I am also asking, and though the authors state that this DNA/data should be shared "within the context of research and discovery," at this point, it is fair to ask if even that is something we are comfortable with, especially given the outcomes of this "research and discovery."

This would include nanotechnology, a favorite of the World Economic Forum. According to Hele Savin, a World Economic Forum Young Scientist, "Nanotech is not an industry in itself, but an enabler across all industries. By manipulating individual atoms and molecules, you can access intermediary states of matter where nature's physical properties have changed; this is unlocking commercial opportunities from health to manufacturing, energy to farming."[95] According to a World Economic Forum piece from 2014, "Selecta Biosciences – like BIND, one of last year's crop of Technology Pioneers – uses nanotech to target immune cells rather than diseased cells. Selecta has designed nanoparticles which dampen the response of the immune system to specified triggers."[96] Is that right? And what might the delivery mechanism of such nanoparticles be, and for what

---

[95] Wright, "How Nanotech Is Changing."
[96] Ibid.

reason? The Forum also states that nanotechnology could "reduce inequality"—more language of liberalism—and "tackle climate change."

This neatly aligns with the current operating model of high finance and global corporations: ESG, or Environmental, Social, and Governance. Investing would fall under some version of "sustainable," "socially responsible," or some similar nice-sounding category that really amounts to degenerate garbage or crippling social mobility and independence. According to the CFA Institute, "As ESG investing accelerates in demand, several key trends are emerging – from climate change to social unrest. The coronavirus pandemic, in particular, has intensified discussions about the interconnectedness of sustainability and the financial system." Legitimate discussions to have, to be sure, but it always turns into some warped version of White supremacy-Christianity-whatever rather than George Soros funding "activist," ideological DAs or Catholic Charities dumping massive amounts of so-called refugees into formerly peaceful and homogeneous areas. We *definitely* should be having a discussion about sustainability and the financial system of neo-liberalism that created so many of these problems in the first place. But instead: "abortions for some, miniature American flags for others."

In practice, these ESG initiatives are a disaster; there are many examples, but one really need look no further than the catastrophe in Sri Lanka. In November 2021, the country announced that it would make ESG and sustainability issues its top priority; the country's central bank also partnered with the International Finance Corporation to launch a "green taxonomy" using the EU's International Platform on Sustainable Finance's Common Ground Taxonomy, which includes "climate smart agricultural activities." Fast forward to May 2022, as *Al Jazeera* reports:

> *Mahinda Samarawickrema, 49, will not be planting paddy this season. After a government ban on chemical fertilisers cut his rice yield in half during the March harvest, the farmer, who owns eight hectares (20 acres) of paddy and banana, said he no longer has the income to maintain a farm. Especially as his banana crop also looks set to fail. . . .*
>
> *An island nation of 22 million people, Sri Lanka used to be self-sufficient in food. But President Gotabaya Rajapaksa's drive to make the country the world's first to fully adopt organic agriculture – by*

banning all synthetic agrochemicals, including fertilisers and pesticides – has proved disastrous for Sri Lanka's food security.

For NPR from the same month:

Sri Lanka is in crisis. There are power blackouts and food shortages. Protests have turned violent. . . . These people, the protesters in Colombo caught them. They were so angry that the prime minister had instigated this violence, so they charged at his residence, and they set fire to the main gate of the prime minister's official residence. And then it turned out to be extremely bad. And they started attacking the current government. Nearly 36 government politicians' residence, offices and some hotels were all set on fire within overnight. . . . This country is penniless. There is no money at the treasury. There is no money to buy food. There is no money to buy fuel. And people are starving.

Now in talks with the IMF about a bailout, the UNDP suggested that perhaps the country could make a "debt for nature swap," which would take the form of debt relief for some kind of conservation measures. That would probably be mostly farmland "reclaimed" by nature. Enter artificially-induced scarcity. This is what it looks like when a country decides to adopt the full-on ESG measures, and the resultant collapse is totally expected, encouraged even. Of course we see the financial and supra-governmental overlords step in, and as is the case with all of these measures designed to be eco-friendly and sustainable, the real motivation is to destroy self-sufficiency. There is nothing wrong with organic growing in and of itself—it's pretty great, in fact—but it is unrealistic to expect a country to flip a switch and be in an Edenic organic paradise in a season. It's unrealistic to expect that to ever happen with the modern world, as it's impossible to sustain the global population, or even the population of one smaller country as we're seeing, without some non-organic inputs. It also doesn't mean we need Franken-plants, but as with many things, there's a happy medium that as usual the ruling class and other assorted ideologues just blow right by. This is the weaponization of food, and it's playing out everywhere. Get people hungry and desperate, and that's when revolutions happen. Here the revolution will lead the Sri Lankans right into the waiting arms of global capital and the globalist/World Economic Forum types. Their suffering will be parlayed into totally ending self-sufficiency with finance, as usual, applying the ultimate leverage.

I'll be blunt: the financial system above all else is *the* problem, with obscure financial instruments, usurious lending, backroom dealing and insiderism, and fiat currency its defining features. None of this happens without the money to corrupt and grease the skids and the access and influence these inflated and often questionable if not ill-gotten gains afford. Let's consider two representative figures: Soros and BlackRock co-founder, Chairman, and CEO Larry Fink. Soros made his fortune as a hedge fund manager (most famously betting against the pound in 1992 when he made $1.5 billion in just one month) and has used his exorbitant wealth to fund the corrosive Open Society Foundations (for more depth on what that looks like in particular, the reader is directed to my book *The Open Society Playbook*).

Fink is on the Board of Trustees of the World Economic Forum and is an Emeritus Board member of the Robin Hood Foundation alongside other wealthy Jews like Steven A. Cohen (discussed earlier), Dirk Ziff (Ziff Capital Partners), and Lloyd Blankfein (Goldman Sachs), as well as Stan Druckenmiller (lead portfolio manager for Soros's Quantum Fund for over a decade), Jewish former CNN President Jeff Zucker, and media fixtures like Brian Williams, Tom Brokaw, and Diane Sawyer. Fink is described by *Financial Times* as "the most powerful person in global finance, a consigliere to presidents and prime ministers and with clout in almost every major corporate boardroom in the world." At the beginning of his career, as Robin Wigglesworth writes:

> *[Fink] went to First Boston . . . where he started working in 1976. . . . Many of his team were Jewish, leading some at the firm to dub Fink's desk "Little Israel. . . ." [Fink would hire] a working-class Wharton graduate from Monticello named Robert Kapito. . . . When Rosh Hashana arrived, it emerged that Kapito was as Jewish as the rest of the desk. . . . Some years earlier, Fink had become phone pals with Ralph Schlosstein, an investment banker at Shearson Lehman Hutton. . . . Both were Democrats — Schlosstein had been a Treasury official in the Carter administration before heading to Wall Street — but mostly they talked about dissatisfaction with their jobs and a hunger to start something new. . . . [During the 2008 financial crisis] BlackRock's prestigious mandates to help the US Treasury and*

the Federal Reserve sort out the detritus of the financial crisis prompted complaints about the company's proximity to power. . . . But it was the 2009 deal to acquire Barclays Global Investors, and the supercharged growth that followed, that propelled Fink to the top of Wall Street.

BlackRock has swollen to its current size as a direct consequence of investments made in particular during the 2008 financial crisis and the 2020 coronavirus upheavals. It is a massive investor in the military-industrial complex, Chinese industry, and ESGs; in 2020, Fink announced that "sustainability" would form a core component of BlackRock's future investment decisions, and that "climate risk" is "compelling investors to reassess core assumptions about modern finance." In his 2020 letter to CEOs entitled "A Fundamental Reshaping of Finance," Fink stated that:

I believe we are on the edge of a fundamental reshaping of finance. . . . In the near future – and sooner than most anticipate – there will be a significant reallocation of capital. . . . Every government, company, and shareholder must confront climate change. . . . Over the next few years, one of the most important questions we will face is the scale and scope of government action on climate change, which will generally define the speed with which we move to a low-carbon economy. This challenge cannot be solved without a coordinated, international response from governments, aligned with the goals of the Paris Agreement. . . . While government must lead the way in this transition, companies and investors also have a meaningful role to play. As part of this responsibility, BlackRock was a founding member of the Task Force on Climate-related Financial Disclosures (TCFD). We are a signatory to the UN's Principles for Responsible Investment, and we signed the Vatican's 2019 statement advocating carbon pricing regimes, which we believe are essential to combating climate change. BlackRock has joined with France, Germany, and global foundations to establish the Climate Finance Partnership, which is one of several public-private efforts to improve financing mechanisms for infrastructure investment. The need is particularly urgent for cities. . . . Given the groundwork we have already laid engaging on disclosure, and the growing investment risks surrounding sustainability, we will be increasingly disposed to vote

*against management and board directors when companies are not
making sufficient progress on sustainability-related disclosures and
the business practices and plans underlying them.*

So there we see, plain as day, Fink outlining the impetus for re-shaping the
global economy in line with the Green New Deal raft of policies. A "de-
carbonized economy" means less for you and me and a dramatic restriction
in our freedom of movement ostensibly to cut down on carbon emissions—
a freedom of movement already severely restricted through various coronavirus measures and staggering price hikes in fossil fuels. If everyone is
on electric, how difficult is it to simply cut the power to the non-compliant? Exactly.

BlackRock is now the world's largest asset manager, and along with
State Street and Vanguard, the "big three" were the largest owners in 88%
of the S&P 500 companies as of 2020. As a result of their influence, situations such as when in 2021 they colluded to back a bid by "activist" firm
Engine No. 1 to stack Exxon Mobil's board with pro-ESG candidates despite
their owning only 0.02 percent of the company's shares will become increasingly prevalent. As we've seen time and again, it is the big money firms
backing true extremists and ideologues such as the Bolsheviks that explains why so often in the modern world the lunatics appear to be running
the asylum. It's the same thing the Open Society Foundations does, just
different mechanisms and pressure points.

There is no daylight between any of these entities, whether it be in
practice, ideology, or actual personnel and funding. Just as George Soros
admitted that the Open Society aims are more or less synonymous with
those of the US State Department, we see something very similar in the
financial realm with that of BlackRock and the US government as well.
Headlines like the following from *The Wall Street Journal* in May 2020
abound, showing the ubiquity and centrality of BlackRock in the US—and
to a large extent global—economy: "Big Money Managers Take Lead Role
in Managing Coronavirus Stimulus" ("BlackRock is about to start buying
billions of dollars in corporate bonds for the Fed"). It seems every time the
house of cards is about to come crashing down, the Federal Reserve runs
to BlackRock to save the day; for Gillian Tett, writing in March 2020 for
Financial Times:

Wall Street watchers might feel as if they are living in Groundhog Day. Now, as in 2008, markets are melting down. . . . Twelve not-so-long years ago, the Fed turned to BlackRock to manage the three Maiden Lane vehicles that it created to hold assets from the defunct insurer AIG and also Bear Stearns. On Tuesday, it again tapped BlackRock's Financial Markets Advisory, its consultancy arm, again to run three vehicles the Fed will create to buy corporate debt from the primary and secondary markets, and also commercial mortgage-backed securities. . . . What is more notable is that BlackRock received this mandate without a contest.

None of the systemic issues that caused the 2008 financial meltdown were ever really resolved; they were effectively papered-over with the can kicked down the road. Why would those who were profiting so immensely from the shell game give it all up? If anything, Wall Street and Washington have become even more incestuous. The trainwreck known as the Biden administration might as well be called the BlackRock administration; Michael Pyle, former global chief investment strategist for BlackRock, is the chief economic advisor to Vice President Kamala Harris. Wally Adeyemo, a former chief of staff to Larry Fink, is with the Treasury Department and former BlackRock investment executive Brian Deese leads Biden's National Economic Council. Deese, Adeyemo, and Pyle also all were a part of the Obama administration. Keep these guys in mind as you pay five dollars a gallon for gas or can't afford groceries. Do the same when you can't afford a house, as BlackRock and JP Morgan Asset Management buy entire residential communities and turn the homes into rental units. Remember: you will own nothing and like it.

The influence of BlackRock is not limited to the United States and the rest of the world only by extension through the US dollar as the world reserve currency. BlackRock has advised the Central Bank of Ireland, Her Majesty's Treasury, and the Bank of Greece, in addition to the Federal Reserve Bank of New York. Friedrich Merz, Leader of the Christian Democratic Union party in Germany, is a former BlackRock executive. BlackRock Board member Hans Vestberg is on the Board of the United Nations Foundation and is a commissioner of the UN-backed Broadband Commission for Sustainable Development, with the mission statement that broadband access is vital to the achievement of the UN's Sustainable Development Goals. You know those Javelin missiles killing Russians in the Ukraine, about which Joe Biden apparently saw some humor in a speech, part of the tens of billions of dollars the US government shelled out for their proxy war there while there's no defense of the border here? They were developed by a joint venture between Raytheon and Lockheed Martin. State Street, Vanguard, and BlackRock are the three largest shareholders of both Raytheon and Lockheed Martin stock.

This is a war where the timing seems eerily impeccable, in much the same way that the George Floyd protests did. Can I say for sure that Russian President Vladimir Putin is in on the game? No, but there is a conjecture to be made. At minimum, the situation has been seized upon by the floundering US government as not so much red meat for their bloodthirsty base who might not be able to slaughter babies wholesale anymore, but let's call it soy for the base, a base that has been propagandized into thinking Putin is Hitler and is responsible for all of what's gone wrong in this country for years. Granted the supply shocks of food and fuel in particular born out of the Ukrainian conflict are real, but the cutting-off of the Western nose to spite its face with regard to Russian oil—particularly in Europe—is very much intentional. The shortages in the US came as a result of the Biden administration mostly shutting down domestic production and on top of that, refinery closures and already-scarce diesel being promised to an energy-starved Europe.

The war is brilliant from a propaganda and dialectical perspective; Russia is back in the mix as the new Cold War foil, and there's now the Next Big Thing to distract from COVID and the continually-encroaching medical tyranny. That has not gone away, but is finding its feet more solidly away from public scrutiny. It is vital that we understand that each of these seemingly disparate situations are deeply intertwined in the same way the global economy was. The shocks play into a larger pain game that is a controlled demolition of the West, which will, if successful, make the technocracy in complete control over literally everything. This is a bipolar world, and I mean that in the multiple senses one could interpret that phrase. Whether it is Russia as the last relative holdout of the system being crushed (Larry Fink in a March 2022 letter to shareholders proudly boasted that "In consultation with our stakeholders, BlackRock has also joined the global effort to isolate Russia from financial markets," and certain Russian banks were cut off from the SWIFT system—remember both SWIFT and BlackRock are World Economic Forum partners) or whether its leadership is intentionally playing the villain, I do not know. What I can say for certain is that the events, like the COVID pandemic, are at minimum being seized upon to further the transhumanist-globalist project. Certainly the changes to the Ukrainian state's digital ID app in the middle of a conflict—and intersecting with the usual jargon of "statelessness" and refugees and all the other familiar talking points (not to diminish the tragedy, but simply to point out the rhetorical devices being used in furtherance of the agenda)—is suspect.

Eventually the so-called "elites" want a currency reset and they want it digitized and tied to social credit scores, personal finances, devices from vehicles to phones, and biometric data; it is a central part of the Internet of All Things, and it will be centrally-controlled. Dissidents will be shut out completely, and that's best case. Given that this is a transhumanist jihad—not a crusade as it is based on apostasy and warped, immoral foundations—"just" being left in the cold is highly unlikely. The CBDC moves and the "sexyifying" of blockchain/cryptocurrencies (before the crypto markets will be destroyed as there cannot be competition) must be understood in this context of total central control. Countries such as the Bahamas and Nigeria have already launched CBDCs; others such as Russia, China, South Africa, Saudi Arabia, and South Korea are piloting CBDCs. The Euro Area, Brazil, Canada, Turkey, Japan, Australia, and India are among those in the development stage, with the US and UK among those in the research stage. This is coming, as 87 countries representing over 90 percent of global GDP are exploring a CBDC.

The program being piloted in the Ukraine is being done in conjunction with the Stellar Development Foundation, operating out of San Francisco. According to Stellar's website, citing runaway inflation:

> The way the global financial establishment is structured today, people are born into an economy just like they're born into a political system. Stellar is a way out: it lets people participate in a worldwide, stable, financial network regardless of where they live. For example, using Stellar, a family in Venezuela can keep some of its savings in dollars, or in euros, and protect itself from local economic upheaval—without having to keep bills "under the mattress" or operate through a gray market broker.

Among their Board of Directors is included Lin-Hua Wu of Google, and the gay Jewish CEO of OpenAI Sam Altman is an advisor. Remember the Peter Thiel- and Elon Musk-backed OpenAI from the Introduction?

Writing in March 2022 to BlackRock shareholders, Larry Fink really quite neatly packaged the whole agenda and its multiple angles of attack and filtered it through the Ukrainian conflict's lens:

> *I am proud of BlackRock's support for refugees fleeing their homes. . . . But the Russian invasion of Ukraine has put an end to the globalization we have experienced over the last three decades. We had already seen connectivity between nations, companies and even people strained by two years of the pandemic. It has left many communities and people feeling isolated and looking inward. I believe this has exacerbated the polarization and extremist behavior we are seeing across society today. The invasion has catalyzed nations and governments to come together to sever financial and business ties with Russia. United in their steadfast commitment to support the Ukrainian people, they launched an "economic war" against Russia. Governments across the world almost unanimously imposed sanctions, including taking the unprecedented step of barring the Russian central bank from deploying its hard currency reserves. Capital markets, financial institutions and companies have gone even further beyond government-imposed sanctions. As I wrote in my letter to CEOs earlier this year, access to capital markets is a privilege, not a right. . . . Russia has been essentially cut off from global capital markets, demonstrating the commitment of major companies to operate consistent with core values. This "economic war" shows what we can achieve when companies, supported by their stakeholders, come together.*

If they can do that to an entire country, one armed with thousands of nuclear warheads, what will they do to *you*? It's cancel culture on steroids. Fink continues:

> *I believe that recent events will actually accelerate the shift toward greener sources of energy in many parts of the world. During the pandemic, we saw how a crisis can act as a catalyst for innovation. Businesses, governments, and scientists came together to develop*

and deploy vaccines at scale in record time. . . . Finally, a less dis-
cussed aspect of the war is its potential impact on accelerating dig-
ital currencies. The war will prompt countries to re-evaluate their
currency dependencies. . . . A global digital payment system *(em-*
phasis added), thoughtfully designed, can enhance the settlement of
international transactions while reducing the risk of money laun-
dering and corruption. Digital currencies can also help bring down
costs of cross-border payments, for example when expatriate work-
ers send earnings back to their families.

One thing you'll notice is other than pinning everything on Putin, there
are no actual attempts at explaining why, for example, a conflict in Eastern
Europe would force "countries to re-evaluate their currency dependencies," unless it's the implied threat of "comply or else." The entire world has
been made to answer to finance, worship it even, and it is the primary vehicle through which the forcible conversion of the globe's people to transhumanism is being used. Even warfare is to a large extent financial.

In his shareholder letter, Fink acknowledged that the three-decade,
post-Cold War, globalization era is over, and in the sense that we can ex-
tend that back to the end of World War II, the Bretton Woods agreement,
and the predominance of neo-liberalism, that is correct. However, globalization as an ideal and aim is not over—far from it. Though we may get this
bipolar world where there is a clear fracture line—at least superficially—
we may find ourselves engineered into an "Oceania has always been at war
with Eastasia" scenario; as Russian Foreign Minister Sergei Lavrov stated
that Russia has been assailed through a "total hybrid war" (true), the country has looked to deepen partnerships on the Asian continent with many
of the Middle Eastern states, China, and India. "The collective West has
declared total hybrid war on us and it is hard to predict how long all this
will last but it is clear the consequences will be felt by everyone, without
exception," Lavrov said. Indeed, the Jewish Representative of Maryland's
8th Congressional District Jamie Raskin has characterized this struggle as
a holy war, one where the evil Russian Orthodox civilization must be destroyed because it has traditional social values:

Democrats like me . . . have passionately supported every package
of military, strategic and economic assistance to the Ukrainian peo-
ple. . . . Ukraine's struggle embodies a democratic future. Its civilian

and military leadership is young and diverse. . . . Its president . . . is Jewish. . . . Moscow right now is . . . a world center of antifeminist, antigay, anti-trans hatred, as well as the homeland of replacement theory for export.

Now is Russia under Putin's leadership "the good guy"? As I mentioned, Putin has a World Economic Forum connection, albeit tenuous, and Russia is one of the countries piloting a CBDC in the digital ruble. Among its technology partners is Sberbank, whose subsidiary BI.ZONE is the organizer of Cyber Polygon supported by the World Economic Forum Centre for Cybersecurity. WEF Centre for Cybersecurity partners include BlackRock, SWIFT, the State Grid Corporation of China, Huawei, and China Huaneng Group. Consider the context of digital IDs and payment systems previously discussed, and then consider former British Prime Minister Tony Blair's comments at Cyber Polygon: "Digital ID for me is a very big part of the future. Inevitably, governments are going to move in this direction — absolutely, inevitably." Does this incontrovertibly prove collusion? No, but rarely are events always as they seem, and we would do well not to take them on face value and in isolation.

Conclusion

"Welcome to the human race." – Snake Plissken

It should be readily apparent by now that the ruling class is beyond redemption in its lunatic designs to fundamentally re-shape humanity and, indeed, the very fabric of reality. While not uniform in its ultimate aims—as possible different factions of slightly competing visions appear to exist—in orientation all endeavor to subjugate the mass of humanity and/or re-engineer it beyond all recognition. This is not the stuff of science fiction, this is reality, and the mad scientists are determining the global agenda with us as their guinea pigs. Creating walking abominations is not being done "for the good of humanity." Is this the future we want for ourselves? It's certainly what the "elites" want. They are incapable of pausing to consider whether just because something can be done, *should* it be done? To quote Dr. Ian Malcolm from *Jurassic Park*, "Your scientists were so preoccupied with whether or not they could, they didn't stop to think if they should." Instead, they are invested in creating a global Panopticon, an artificial intelligence overlord with whom they aim to merge, and untold other hybrids and horrors (such as scientists in Japan growing a human ear on the back of a rat using stem cells).

These self-styled masters of humanity are, quite literally in fact, trying to play God, from the scripting of reality, to artificial intelligence, to cloning, and even creating chimeras. As Nicoletta Lanese reported in August 2019 for *The Scientist*:

An international team of researchers has created embryos contain-
ing both human and monkey cells. . . . The controversial project was
conducted in China, rather than in the US where the project leader
is based, "to avoid legal issues," according to the newspaper [El
País], and ultimately aims to grow viable organs for transplantation
into humans. Juan Carlos Izpisúa Belmonte of the Salk Institute in
San Diego is spearheading the project with scientists from his own
lab and those from the Murcia Catholic University in Murcia, Spain.
The team wants to develop chimeras—organisms composed of cells
from two or more species—capable of growing human organs. . . .
In July, Japanese researchers—including Hiromitsu Nakauchi of the
University of Tokyo and Stanford University—first received permis-
sion from the government to create human-animal embryos to be
transplanted into surrogates.

It would be so easy to dismiss all of this as mere conspiratorial junk, which the media apparatus is quick to do. It's conspiratorial, yes, but in word and deed it's happening. Whether it's biolabs in the Ukraine, China, or Connecticut, whatever the plausible deniability, biowarfare is being at minimum explored by multiple parties and more than likely has been launched on more than one occasion. Auto-immune diseases such as Lyme and HIV/AIDS are very recent phenomena, and both proliferated at around the same time in around the same geographic region. Supposedly HIV/AIDS comes from the heart of the Dark Continent, but supposedly Lyme disease didn't come from the Plum Island Animal Disease Center. COVID-19 is an artificially-created virus with HIV inserts; this naturally begs the question: why are the "elites" so hell-bent on destroying our natural defenses? Think about this: n-acetyl cysteine (NAC) is a remarkably effective natural supplement that is used by the body to build glutathione, a powerful antioxidant; NAC has anti-inflammatory and immune-modulating characteristics that have shown great promise in the treatment and prevention of COVID-19. There is anecdotal evidence that it has proven beneficial in the treatment of Lyme disease as well and is generally a very helpful supplement in boosting immune function. As a result, the FDA decided to declare it a drug as the sale of pharmaceuticals as supplements is in most instances illegal. This is reminiscent of the way that the safe and effective ivermectin was marginalized in its treatment of COVID-19 in favor of treatments that probably increased the initial death toll on purpose. Now it's all vaccines,

vaccines, vaccines, and as we've established, for COVID-19, *they're not even vaccines* outside of the Orwellian re-definition.

As regards the "vaccines" in particular, there is some discussion that they may in fact be the delivery system for the necessary material for humans to become integrated with Klaus Schwab's Internet of Things/Internet of Bodies, with humans and their devices no longer fully separate entities. I must stipulate here that this is at present conjecture and should be treated as a hypothesis. It is, however, a compelling one that bears further research and consideration. Certainly, at minimum, we are right to question the heavy push for injecting the totality of the population where such a scheme is logically and medically unwarranted for a relatively benign virus, one that, despite promises of Christmas for good behavior, is being positioned to forever be the boot stomping on humanity's face—provided humanity doesn't merge with its machines. What is clearly not benign are the designs of the "elites."

It is possible that the immunosuppressive qualities of the "vaccines" are a by-product of needing a weakened immune system so as to not reject what's being carried within the injections. The connections to HIV/AIDS research and the figures involved (such as Anthony Fauci) raise major alarms as well. It may well be a calculated risk that some large percentage of people will die on the way to "upgrading" humanity. It may also be "just" that COVID-19 is the best opportunity for direct control the "elites" have been presented with, and they are running with it. It has been decided, for whatever reason, that the time is now, and the acceleration is on.

The World Health Organization has stated that coronavirus is pretty much here to stay and has used the pandemic to push for legislation commonly referred to as a "pandemic treaty." As Ilona Kickbusch and Haik Nikogosian of the Global Health Centre at the Graduate Institute of International and Development Studies in Geneva wrote about such a treaty in 2021:

> *Needs to strengthen existing institutions such as the World Health Organization (WHO) and provide it with more authority. . . . it must also look beyond health—and already some of the health-related issues mentioned above cannot be resolved without multisectoral action, for example, take production or supply chains. The social and economic disruptions caused by pandemics are enormous; the future treaty cannot fulfil expectations without addressing a*

range of issues such as international movements and transport, fiscal measures, international trade, social protection, jobs and education. . . . [The treaty] might also link compliance to treaty privileges, trade, or monetary measures.

Sounds a lot like Larry Fink's open letter about Russia, doesn't it?

The aim is for such a treaty under the auspices of the World Health Organization to be adopted by 2024, and as the European Council states, such a treaty would be legally binding under international law. The Council adopted in May 2021 a decision to support the launch of negotiations for an international agreement on "the fight against pandemics within the framework of WHO." In February of that year, the Council declared it wants "to make best use of big data and digital technologies for medical research and healthcare" and that "We are committed to advancing global health security, including by strengthening the World Health Organization and working towards an international treaty on pandemics within its framework." Would it include "better surveillance"? It would. "Universal and equitable access to medical solutions, such as vaccines"? Yup. "A stronger international health framework with the WHO as the coordinating authority on global health matters" and a "One Health approach, connecting the health of humans, animals and our planet"? Yes and yes. The European Union also wants to "create a framework which could obligate digital services to use automated technologies," ostensibly to scan for child sexual abuse material, but let's be honest: it's to monitor communications and snuff out dissent. Combatting child abuse and molestation is literally the *last* thing the "elites" care about, trust me.

In addition to keeping tabs on you, they also want more data for their piggy algorithms. For example, Purdue University's Synthetic Environment for Analysis and Simulations (SEAS) is an "engine that enables researchers and organizations to try out their models or techniques" and is used by the Sentient World Simulation (SWS), a "synthetic mirror of the real world with automated continuous calibration with respect to current real-world information." This parallel "real world" is continuously fed data in order to create the most realistic simulated world possible, and then to run various scenarios through it in order to war game/project scenarios and outcomes. According to Alok R. Chaturvedi, who directs Purdue's laboratories for Synthetic Environment for Analysis and Simulations: "Within the synthetic world are models of individuals, organizations, institutions, infrastructure, and geographies that represent the traits and mimic the behaviors of their corresponding real world counterparts." As Mark Baard wrote in 2007 for *The Register*:

> [T]he US Department of Defense (DOD) may already be creating a copy of you in an alternate reality to see how long you can go without food or water, or how you will respond to televised propaganda.
>
> The DOD is developing a parallel to Planet Earth, with billions of individual "nodes" to reflect every man, woman, and child this side of the dividing line between reality and AR called the Sentient World Simulation (SWS). . . .
>
> "SWS provides an environment for testing Psychological Operations (PSYOP)," [a paper for the project] reads, so that military leaders can "develop and test multiple courses of action to anticipate and shape behaviors of adversaries, neutrals, and partners."
>
> SWS also replicates financial institutions, utilities, media outlets, and street corner shops. By applying theories of economics and human psychology, its developers believe they can predict how individuals and mobs will respond to various stressors.
>
> Yank a country's water supply. Stage a military coup. SWS will tell you what happens next. . . .
>
> The Joint Innovation and Experimentation Directorate of the US Joint Forces Command (JFCOM-J9) in April began working with Homeland Security and multinational forces over "Noble Resolve 07", a homeland defense experiment.
>
> In August, the agencies will shift their crises scenarios from the East Coast to the Pacific theatre.
>
> JFCOM-J9 completed another test of SEAS last year. Called Urban Resolve, the experiment projected warfare scenarios for Baghdad in 2015, eight years from now.
>
> JFCOM-9 is now capable of running real-time simulations for up to 62 nations, including Iraq, Afghanistan, and China. The simulations gobble up breaking news, census data, economic indicators, and climactic events in the real world, along with proprietary information such as military intelligence.
>
> Military and intel officials can introduce fictitious agents into the simulations (such as a spike in unemployment, for example) to gauge their destabilising effects on a population. . . .

> *[Jim Blank, modelling and simulation division chief at JFCOM-J9 said,]* "*Future wars will be asymmetric in nature. They will be more non-kinetic, with the center of gravity being a population. . . .*"
> "*(SWS) is a hungry beast,*" *Blank said.*

Chaturvedi has a commercial version available through his company Simulex, and its major clients have included the pharmaceutical heavy Eli Lilly and defense contractor Lockheed Martin.

We know that already in 2006, the aforementioned Blank co-authored a paper stating that:

> *Multinational experimentation is a critical element of the United States Joint Forces Command's (USJFCOM) Experimentation Directorate (J9) joint concept development and experimentation program. The Multinational Experiment (MNE) series explores ways to achieve a coalition's political goals by influencing the behaviour of our adversaries by relying on the full weight of the coalition's collective national powers (diplomatic, information, military and economics actions). MNE4, conducted in February – March 2006, was one such experimentation venue that explored new ways to apply the various elements of the coalition's considerable influence, short of direct military conflict. MNE4 required an extensive international modeling and simulation (M&S) development effort with models provided by France, Germany and the United States. . . .*
>
> *The United States provided the Joint Semi-Automated Forces (JSAF) and the Synthetic Environment for Analysis and Simulation (SEAS) systems. . . .*
>
> *The MNE4 participants [were] Australia, Canada, Finland, France, Germany, Sweden, the United Kingdom, the North Atlantic Treaty Organization (NATO) and the United States.*

We now find ourselves in the midst of the dense fog of war, with NATO clearly agitating for one with Russia and its satellites; the Ukrainian people are unfortunately caught in the middle, as the regular folks always are, their country used as a staging-ground for what may well be designed to expand into a global conflict. Is Russia playing its part in the game, or has it finally decided to break out of the neo-liberal constraints imposed upon its ambitions? The situation that began in the Ukraine isn't "just" Vietnam or some other proxy war, although that is true. The expansion of NATO and the intentional staging of war games right in Russia's backyard (such as Steadfast Defender 21 in the Black Sea in 2021, involving 9,000 troops from twenty nations or those in Estonia in 2022, involving 15,000 troops from ten countries including the US, the Ukraine, Finland, and Sweden—to say nothing of overt US and NATO military funding of the Ukraine and openly bragging about using intelligence to assassinate Russian generals and sink Russian ships) signals as much.

There are a variety of possibilities for why such a war "must" happen, from the Western leadership perspective: it obscures lots of questions and deaths surrounding COVID and its "vaccines" more specifically; it gets rid of plenty of pesky people for more transhumanist *lebensraum*; it destroys a rival economic model in Russia the same as was done to post-Weimar Germany and 1990s Yugoslavia; it creates a *1984* "we've always been at war with Eastasia"-type scenario and solidifies superficially-competing blocs; it creates fear and thus allows for easier social control; it serves as a trial balloon for the domestic application of total asymmetric/fifth generation warfare (which is already being applied to a very large extent at home); and wars are often used as a useful shuffling of the deck as it were where debts can be erased or incurred and fortunes can be made. You could also end up triggering something so devastating *that* ends up as your reset. I won't pretend to have all the answers as I am not privy to those conversations, obviously, but we can speculate.

Given what we've just discussed about the constant simulations and war-gaming, with the advancements in artificial intelligence and other enabling technologies and infrastructure, it's entirely possible all of this is being stage-managed to effectuate the Great Reset on the Grand Chessboard. With the other emerging crises set very likely to intersect, and the speed and coordination with which this has occurred, it is very difficult not to at least suspect that a massively disruptive war would be the coup de grace for the "liberal world order" we must suffer massive inflation and economic destruction for. The agricultural shortfalls caused by the Russian invasion of the Ukraine at a time of global artificially-induced scarcity of crops, coupled with the insistence on corn production in the United States to be directed even more so toward ethanol ostensibly to alleviate sky-high gas prices, should have more than a few eyebrows raised.

We have become so siloed in our thinking, so reactive in the face of rapid-fire "shiny object" stimuli, bombarded by propaganda, that most simply cannot see what is playing out before them in otherwise fairly obvious ways. It is my hope that through illustrating the connections between organizations and other entities acting in concert, in showing those instances where the transhumanists actually speak frankly about their motivations and desires, and in how their arrogance can occasion a slip of the mask—to say nothing of the curious impulse to symbolically sign-post—that we can gain awareness of the agenda that's been set in motion and act accordingly. The informed observer should note that this is a war that is not like any other war, really, as it is for all the marbles. World War III is a battle for the soul of humanity.

Regardless of what institutional or state actors emerge victorious in this war—whether it's a genuine conflict at all or merely kabuki theater—we lose. The human element is already being erased, be it in China, where everything is tracked and traced and artificial intelligence "aiding" the Supreme People's Court in Beijing can overturn verdicts "tainted by human mistake," or in the United States, where "The National AI Initiative Act of 2020 (DIVISION E, SEC. 5001) became law on January 1, 2021, providing for a coordinated program across the entire Federal government to accelerate AI research and application for the Nation's economic prosperity and national security." It is a future that envisions the obsolescence of humanity, moving on to something faster and more efficient, possibly more self-indulgent but certainly something that makes us lesser, not greater. This is again assuming the artificial intelligence does not dispense with humanity altogether, despite the vain hopes that the transhumanists might merge with their AI creation and god.

The transhumanists' vision is a perverse one, inverting that which is true and timeless; the answers to the questions that should be asked remain unconsidered as they are obscured by the fervent work to unmake humanity in the quest to re-make it. The perfect is the enemy of the good, as it were, as the secular materialists' notion that man can be his own god building monuments to himself becomes inexorably transformed into the creator worshipping his creation. The closer one gets to the essence of what *is*, the more one begins to see the paradoxical nature of that which defines us. To be or not to be, that is, in fact, the question. For the transhumanists, what promises salvation can only end in destruction. There is wisdom is differentiating between *could* and *should*, in knowing what answers to seek and what should remain a mystery. The secrets of the universe aren't hidden in some black box. They aren't in summoning intelligences vastly superior to ours whose purposes will be inscrutable and whose care for us may kindly be referred to as that of a man for an ant in his kitchen. If you value liberty and human sovereignty—if you believe you have a soul and it is valuable—then it is incumbent upon you to resist this agenda with all your might. We all must.

Bibliography

Introduction

Gillis, Alexander S. "What is the internet of things (IoT?" Tech Target. Accessed November 14, 2022. https://www.techtarget.com/iotagenda/definition/Internet-of-Things-IoT.

McGinnis, Devon. "What Is the Fourth Industrial Revolution?" *Salesforce*, October 27, 2020. https://www.salesforce.com/blog/what-is-the-fourth-industrial-revolution-4ir/.

Schnall, Flora. "Fm-2030." Interview by Noah Adams. *All Things Considered*, NPR, July 11, 2000. Audio, 3:48. https://www.npr.org/2000/07/11/1076532/fm-2030.

Schwab, Klaus. "Now Is the Time for a 'Great Reset.'" World Economic Forum, June 3, 2020. https://www.weforum.org/agenda/2020/06/now-is-the-time-for-a-great-reset/.

Schwab, Klaus and Thierry Malleret. *COVID-19: The Great Reset*. Geneva: Forum Publishing, 2020.

Chapter One

Auken, Ida. "Welcome to 2030: I Own Nothing, Have No Privacy and Life Has Never Been Better." *Forbes Magazine*, November 10, 2016. https://www.forbes.com/sites/worldeconomicforum/2016/11/10/shopping-i-cant-really-remember-what-that-is-or-how-differently-well-live-in-2030/?sh=623fda1c1735.

Derysh, Igor. "Trump's new coronavirus vaccine czar owns $10 million in stock options in company developing vaccine." *Salon*, May 18, 2020. https://www.salon.com/2020/05/18/trumps-new-coronavirus-vaccine-czar-owns-10-million-in-stock-options-in-company-developing-vaccine/.

Gates, Bill. Interview by David Rubenstein. *The David Rubenstein Show: Peer-to-Peer Conversations*, Bloomberg, June 24, 2019. Video, 24:06. https://www.youtube.com/watch?v=zPclQ5GLQFM.

Goldberg, Yair, Micha Mandel, Yinon M. Bar-On, Omri Bodenheimer, Laurence S. Freedman, Nachman Ash, Sharon Alroy-Preis, Amit Huppert, and Ron Milo.

"Protection and Waning of Natural and Hybrid Immunity to SARS-CoV-2." *The New England Journal of Medicine* 386 (June 2022): 2201–12. DOI: 10.1056/NEJMoa2118946.

Harari, Yuval Noah. *Homo Deus: A Brief History of Tomorrow*. London: Harper, 2018.

"JBS Partners with the World Economic Forum to Discuss Climate Change." *JBS Global News*, April 28, 2021. https://www.jbsglobal.co.uk/news/2021/04/jbs-partners-with-the-world-economic-forum-to-discuss-climate-change/.

Klein, Naomi. "Screen New Deal." *The Intercept*, May 8, 2020. https://theintercept.com/2020/05/08/andrew-cuomo-eric-schmidt-coronavirus-tech-shock-doctrine/.

Knoepfler, Paul. "Global transhumanism leader Natasha Vita-More on human germline modification." *The Niche*, August 3, 2015. https://ipscell.com/2015/08/vita-more/.

Kosoff, Maya. "Peter Thiel Wants to Inject Himself with Young People's Blood." *Vanity Fair*, August 1, 2016. https://www.vanityfair.com/news/2016/08/peter-thiel-wants-to-inject-himself-with-young-peoples-blood.

Liptak, Kevin, Jim Acosta, and Kaitlan Collins. "White House names heads of 'warp speed' coronavirus vaccine effort." CNN, May 13, 2020. https://edition.cnn.com/2020/05/13/politics/white-house-coronavirus-vaccine/index.html.

Metz, Cade. "Inside OpenAI, Elon Musk's Wild Plan to Set Artificial Intelligence Free." *Wired*, April 27, 2016. https://www.wired.com/2016/04/openai-elon-musk-sam-altman-plan-to-set-artificial-intelligence-free/.

More, Max. "Extropianism." Extropy Institute and Extropy Journal, January 5, 1996. http://www.mit.edu/people/jpbonsen/extropianism.html.

Philipkoski, Kristen. "Ray Kurzweil's Plan: Never Die." *Wired*, November 18, 2002. https://www.wired.com/2002/11/ray-kurzweils-plan-never-die/.

Rennie, John. "The Immortal Ambitions of Ray Kurzweil: A Review of Transcendent Man." *Scientific American*, February 15, 2011. https://www.scientificamerican.com/article/the-immortal-ambitions-of-ray-kurzweil/#.

Tan, Emily. "Why Cities Are at the Heart of Our Journey towards Net Zero." World Economic Forum, February 23, 2021. https://www.weforum.org/agenda/2021/02/cities-are-at-the-heart-of-our-journey-to-net-zero/.

Vita-More, Natasha. "The Transhumanist Manifesto." Humanity+, 2020. https://www.humanityplus.org/the-transhumanist-manifesto.

Wiener, Anna. "Inside the Tech Industry's Obsession with Immortality." *The New Republic*, February 16, 2017. https://newrepublic.com/article/140260/human.

Wilson, Cintra, "Droid Rage." *The New York Times*, October 21, 2007. https://www.nytimes.com/2007/10/21/style/tmagazine/21droid.html.

World Economic Forum. "A cyber-attack with COVID-like characteristics?" January 18, 2021. YouTube video, 1:41. https://www.youtube.com/watch?v=-ooZA1B300I.

Yuval Noah Harari. "Dr. Yuval Noah Harari - Data Processing - Part 1." 26:50. April 18, 2013. YouTube video, 47:11. https://www.youtube.com/watch?v=6VJMYWKH-W8&t=1590s.

Chapter Two

Assange, Julian. "Assange: Google Is Not What It Seems." *Newsweek*, October 23, 2014. https://www.newsweek.com/assange-google-not-what-it-seems-279447.

"Biological Threat Reduction Program." U.S. Embassy in Ukraine, March 10, 2022.
https://ua.usembassy.gov/embassy/kyiv/sections-offices/defense-threat-reduction-
office/biological-threat-reduction-program/.

"Event 201, a Pandemic Exercise to Illustrate Preparedness Efforts." Johns Hopkins Center
for Health Security, October 18, 2019.
https://www.centerforhealthsecurity.org/event201/.

Greenwald, Glenn. "Victoria Nuland: Ukraine Has 'Biological Research Facilities,' Worried
Russia May Seize Them." Substack, March 9, 2022.
https://greenwald.substack.com/p/victoria-nuland-ukraine-has-biological?s=r.

Reyes, Al. *A Partner in Shaping History (1971–2020)*. World Economic Forum, 2019.
https://www3.weforum.org/docs/WEF_A_Partner_in_Shaping_History.pdf.

Warsh, David. "In Which, at Last, We Meet, Perhaps, Andrei Shleifer's Evil Twin." *Economic
Principals*, April 16, 2006.
http://www.economicprincipals.com/issues/2006.04.16/195.html.

"Watch: Jacinda Ardern Admits New Zealand Will Become a Two-Tier Society over
Vaccines." The Independent. Independent Digital News and Media, October 25, 2021.
https://www.independent.co.uk/tv/news/new-zealand-jacinda-ardern-coronavirus-
vaccines-ve5572e26.

"WEF GLT Class of 1993." World Economic Forum, 1993.
https://web.archive.org/web/20131203013754/http://www3.weforum.org/docs/WEF_GL
T_ClassOf1993.pdf.

"WEF GLT Class of 1995." World Economic Forum, 1995.
https://web.archive.org/web/20140915002450/http://www3.weforum.org/docs/WEF_G
LT_ClassOf1995.pdf.

"WEF GLT Class of 1996." World Economic Forum, 1996.
https://web.archive.org/web/20140915002450/http://www3.weforum.org/docs/WEF_G
LT_ClassOf1996.pdf.

Chapter Three

Bilefsky, Dan. "My Night in a Quarantine Hotel." *The New York Times*, June 18, 2021.
https://www.nytimes.com/2021/06/18/world/canada/toronto-quarantine-hotel.html.

Bloom, Douglas. "Could this COVID-19 'health passport' be the future of travel and events?"
World Economic Forum, July 30, 2020.
https://www.weforum.org/agenda/2020/07/covid-19-passport-app-health-travel-
covidpass-quarantine-event/.

Borak, Masha. "Chinese scientist wants a new Skynet-like system just for tracking viruses."
Abacus, May 22, 2020. https://www.scmp.com/abacus/tech/article/3085543/chinese-
scientist-wants-new-skynet-system-just-tracking-viruses.

"CBD Focus Areas – Biosurveillance." Department of Homeland Security, updated January 7,
2022. https://www.dhs.gov/science-and-technology/biosurveillance.

Clinton, Hillary. "A National Security Reckoning: How Washington Should Think About
Power." *Foreign Affairs*, November/December 2020.
https://www.foreignaffairs.com/articles/united-states/2020-10-09/hillary-clinton-
national-security-reckoning.

Cross, Ryan. "Will the Coronavirus Help MRNA and DNA Vaccines Prove Their Worth?" *Chemical & Engineering News*, April 3, 2020. https://cen.acs.org/pharmaceuticals/vaccines/coronavirus-help-mRNA-DNA-vaccines/98/i14.

Department of Homeland Security. "Summary of Terrorism Threat to the U.S. Homeland." National Terrorism Advisory System Bulletin, August 13, 2021. https://www.dhs.gov/ntas/advisory/national-terrorism-advisory-system-bulletin-august-13-2021.

Edwards, Jim. "Pfizer Bribed Nigerian Officials in Fatal Drug Trial, Ex-Employee Claims." *CBS News*, February 10, 2011. https://www.cbsnews.com/news/pfizer-bribed-nigerian-officials-in-fatal-drug-trial-ex-employee-claims/.

"Event 201, a Pandemic Exercise to Illustrate Preparedness Efforts." Johns Hopkins Center for Health Security, October 18, 2019. https://www.centerforhealthsecurity.org/event201/.

"Event 201 Pandemic Exercise Underscores Immediate Need for Global Public-Private Cooperation to Mitigate Severe Economic and Societal Impacts of Pandemics." Johns Hopkins Center for Health Security, Event 201 Press Release, October 17, 2019. https://www.centerforhealthsecurity.org/event201/191017-press-release.html.

Follmann, Dean, Holly E. Janes, Olive D. Buhule, Honghong Zhou, Bethany Girard, Kristen Marks, Karen Kotloff, et al. "Anti-Nucleocapsid Antibodies Following SARS-COV-2 Infection in the Blinded Phase of the MRNA-1273 COVID-19 Vaccine Efficacy Clinical Trial." medRxiv, April 19, 2022. https://doi.org/10.1101/2022.04.18.22271936.

Greene, Jenna. "Wait What? FDA Wants 55 Years to Process FOIA Request over Vaccine Data." *Reuters*, November 18, 2021. https://www.reuters.com/legal/government/wait-what-fda-wants-55-years-process-foia-request-over-vaccine-data-2021-11-18/.

Hinchcliffe, Tim. "A Skeptical Look at the 'Great Reset': A Technocratic Agenda That Waited Years for a Global Crisis to Exploit." *The Sociable*, November 2, 2020. https://sociable.co/technology/skeptical-great-reset-technocratic-agenda-waited-years-crisis-exploit/.

Horowitz, Daniel. "NIH Study Finds Those with Shots Had Fewer n Antibodies Even after COVID Infection." *Blaze Media*, April 28, 2022. https://www.theblaze.com/op-ed/nih-covid-shots-antibodies.

"Inside Australia's Covid internment camp." Unheard News, December 2, 2021, https://unherd.com/thepost/inside-australias-covid-internment-camp/.

Janofsky, Michael November. "Who Is Tal Zaks, Developer of Moderna's COVID-19 Vaccine?" *Forward*, November 17, 2020. https://forward.com/news/458670/who-is-tal-zaks-developer-of-modernas-covid-19-vaccine/.

Lerner, Sharon and Mara Hvistendahl. "New Details Emerge about Coronavirus Research at Chinese Lab." *The Intercept*, September 6, 2021. https://theintercept.com/2021/09/06/new-details-emerge-about-coronavirus-research-at-chinese-lab/.

Loe, Megan. "Yes, the CDC Changed Its Definition of Vaccine to Be 'More Transparent.'" *King5*, February 7, 2022. https://www.king5.com/article/news/verify/coronavirus-verify/cdc-changed-vaccine-definition-more-transparent/536-03ce7891-2604-4090-b548-b1618d286834.

Love, James. "Moderna and US Government Funding of Its COVID-19 Vaccine Candidate." Knowledge Ecology International, May 21, 2020. https://www.keionline.org/33150.

"Merck Manipulated the Science about the Drug Vioxx." Union of Concerned Scientists, October 12, 2017. https://www.ucsusa.org/resources/merck-manipulated-science-about-drug-vioxx.

Moderna Inc. "Building The Digital Biotech Company: Why and How Digitization is Mission-Critical for Moderna." June 2017. https://dev.modernatx.com/sites/default/files/Moderna_The_Digital_Biotech_Company_White_Paper_6.22.17_FINAL.pdf.

Moderna Inc. "mRNA Vaccines: Disruptive Innovation in Vaccination." May 2017. https://axelkra.us/wp-content/uploads/2020/12/RNA_Vaccines_White_Paper_Moderna_050317_v8_4.pdf.

Nussenzweig, Michel C. "Natural Infection versus Vaccination: Differences in COVID Antibody Responses Emerge." Rockefeller University, August 24, 2021. https://www.rockefeller.edu/news/30919-natural-infection-versus-vaccination-differences-in-covid-antibody-responses-emerge/.

Pradhan, Prashant, Ashutosh Kumar Pandey, Akhilesh Mishra, Parul Gupta, Praveen Kumar Tripathi, Manoj Balakrishnan Menon, James Gomes, Perumal Vivekanandan, and Bishwajit Kundu. "Uncanny Similarity of Unique Inserts in the 2019-Ncov Spike Protein to HIV-1 gp120 and Gag." bioRxiv, January 1, 2020. https://www.biorxiv.org/content/10.1101/2020.01.30.927871v1.

Rabin, Roni Caryn. "Nearly All Patients Hospitalized with COVID-19 Had Chronic Health Issues, Study Finds." *The New York Times*, April 23, 2020. https://www.nytimes.com/2020/04/23/health/coronavirus-patients-risk.html.

Rathi, Akshat, and Adam Pasick. "Chinese researchers have genetically modified a human embryo—and many scientists think they've gone too far." *Quartz*, April 23, 2015. https://qz.com/389494/chinese-researchers-are-the-first-to-genetically-modify-a-human-embryo-and-many-scientists-think-theyve-gone-too-far.

Schwab, Klaus. *The Fourth Industrial Revolution*. World Economic Forum, 2016.

Servick, Kelly. "This Mysterious $2 Billion Biotech Is Revealing the Secrets behind Its New Drugs and Vaccines." *Science*, February 1, 2017. https://www.science.org/content/article/mysterious-2-billion-biotech-revealing-secrets-behind-its-new-drugs-and-vaccines.

Sharma, Vaishali Basu. "Sars-cov2 Is a Chimera With HIV Gene Manipulation." Policy Perspectives Foundation, n.d. https://ppf.org.in/opinion/sars-cov2-is-a-chimera-with-hiv-gene-manipulation.

The White House. "National Strategy for Biosurveillance." July 2012. https://obamawhitehouse.archives.gov/sites/default/files/National_Strategy_for_Biosurveillance_July_2012.pdf.

Zinberg, Joel. "Letter Confirms Wuhan Lab's COVID-19 Leak Was Funded by US Taxpayers." *New York Post*, November 4, 2021. https://nypost.com/2021/11/04/letter-confirms-wuhan-lab-virus-study-was-funded-by-taxpayers/.

Chapter Four

9/11 Commission. *The 9/11 Commission Report: Final Report of the National Commission on Terrorist attacks upon the United States.* New York: WW Norton and Company, 2004.

Blakney, Anna K, and Linda-Gail Bekker. "DNA vaccines join the fight against COVID-19." *The Lancet* 399, no. 10332 (April 2022): 1281–1282. https://doi.org/10.1016%2FS0140-6736(22)00524-4.

Broze, Derrick. "Joe Biden's Coronavirus Task Force Is a Rockefeller, Council on Foreign Relations, Gates Foundation Swamp." *The Last American Vagabond*, November 10, 2020. https://www.thelastamericanvagabond.com/joe-bidens-coronavirus-task-force-is-a-rockefeller-council-on-foreign-relations-gates-foundation-swamp/.

Chudley, Jody. "REVEALED: Facebook's CIA Connections..." *St. Paul Research*. March 29, 2018. https://web.archive.org/web/20200503104231/https://stpaulresearch.com/2018/03/29/revealed-facebooks-cia-connections/.

Clark, Greg, Matt Hancock, Wendy Hall, and Jerome Pesenti. "AI Sector Deal." GOV.UK, May 21, 2019. https://www.gov.uk/government/publications/artificial-intelligence-sector-deal/ai-sector-deal.

"Cyber Polygon," World Economic Forum. Archived November 23, 2020. https://archive.ph/raW6U.

C-Span. "Universal Flu Vaccination." October 29, 2019. Video, 58:39. https://www.c-span.org/video/?465845-1%2Funiversal-flu-vaccine.

"DNA Vaccines." World Health Organization. Accessed October 12, 2022. https://www.who.int/teams/health-product-policy-and-standards/standards-and-specifications/vaccines-quality/dna.

Duffy, Kate. "Billionaire Leon Black paid at least $50 million to Jeffrey Epstein despite claiming the two men had a 'limited relationship,' according to an NYT report." Insider, October 12, 2020. https://www.businessinsider.com/leon-black-paid-50-million-to-jeffrey-epstein-nyt-2020-10.

Durán, Juan Manuel, and Karin Rolanda Jongsma. "Who Is Afraid of Black Box Algorithms? On the Epistemological and Ethical Basis of Trust in Medical Ai." *Journal of Medical Ethics* 47, no. 5 (May 2021): 329–335. http://dx.doi.org/10.1136/medethics-2020-106820.

Hall, Wendy, and Jerome Pesenti. *Growing the Artificial Intelligence Industry in the UK.* 2017. https://assets.publishing.service.gov.uk/government/uploads/system/uploads/attachment_data/file/652097/Growing_the_artificial_intelligence_industry_in_the_UK.pdf.

Harari, Yuval Noah. *Homo Deus: A Brief History of Tomorrow.* New York: Harper, 2017.

Harari, Yuval Noah. *Sapiens: A Brief History of Humankind.* New York: Harper, 2015.

Ketcham, Christopher. "An Israeli Trojan Horse." *Counter Punch*, September 27, 2008. https://www.counterpunch.org/2008/09/27/an-israeli-trojan-horse/.

Madzou, Lofred, Michael Costigan, and Kate MacDonald. "Reimagining Regulation for the Age of AI: New Zealand Pilot Project." World Economic Forum, June 2020. https://www3.weforum.org/docs/WEF_Reimagining_Regulation_Age_AI_2020.pdf.

Montgomery, Stuart. "What's in an Algorithm? The Problem of the Black Box." *Tufts Observer*, February 25, 2019. https://tuftsobserver.org/whats-in-an-algorithm-the-problem-of-the-black-box/.

Nozomi Networks. "Nozomi Networks Announces Strong Growth and New Funding in the First Half of 2020." Nozomi Networks, July 14, 2020. https://www.nozominetworks.com/press-release/nozomi-networks-announces-strong-growth-and-new-funding/.

Rao, Anand, and Kay Firth-Butterfield. "3 Ways COVID-19 Is Transforming Advanced Analytics and Ai." World Economic Forum, July 23, 2020.

https://www.weforum.org/agenda/2020/07/3-ways-covid-19-is-transforming-advanced-analytics-and-ai.

Rao, Anand, and Kay Firth-Butterfield. "Lessons from COVID-19 Modeling: The Interplay of Data, Models and Behaviour." World Economic Forum, May 12, 2020. https://www.weforum.org/agenda/2020/05/covid-19-coronavirus-models-data-behaviour-infection-death-rate-flatten-curve-policy/.

Reuters Staff. "No COVID-19 Vaccine, No Normal Life, UK Minister Suggests." *Reuters*, November 30, 2020. https://www.reuters.com/article/uk-health-coronavirus-britain-vaccines/no-covid-19-vaccine-no-normal-life-uk-minister-suggests-idUSKBN28A24R.

Rivers Caitlin, Martin Elena, Watson Crystal, Schoch-Spana Monica, Cicero Anita, and Inglesby Tom. *Resetting Our Response: Changes Needed in the US Approach to COVID-19*. Baltimore, MD: Johns Hopkins Center for Health Security, 2020. https://www.centerforhealthsecurity.org/our-work/publications/resetting-our-response-changes-needed-in-the-us-approach-to-covid-19.

Rodin, Judith, and Peter Schwartz. *Scenarios for the Future of Technology and International Development*. The Rockefeller Foundation and Global Business Network, 2010. .

Rudin, Cynthia, and Joanna Radin. "Why Are We Using Black Box Models in AI When We Don't Need to? A Lesson from an Explainable AI Competition · Issue 1.2, Fall 2019." *Harvard Data Science Review* 1, no. 2 (November 2019). https://doi.org/10.1162/99608f92.5a8a3a3d.

Shachtman, Noah, "Exclusive: Google, CIA Invest in 'Future' of Web Monitoring." *Wired*, July 28, 2010. https://www.wired.com/2010/07/exclusive-google-cia/.

"Shaping the Future of Technology Governance: Artificial Intelligence and Machine Learning." World Economic Forum. Accessed October 12, 2022. https://www.weforum.org/platforms/shaping-the-future-of-technology-governance-artificial-intelligence-and-machine-learning/.

"Shaping the Future of Urban Transformation." World Economic Forum. Accessed October 12, 2022. https://www.weforum.org/platforms/shaping-the-future-of-the-internet-of-things-and-urban-transformation.

Sigalos, MacKenzie. "Yes, your boss can fire you if you refuse to get a Covid vaccine." CNBC, December 7, 2020. https://www.cnbc.com/2020/12/07/covid-vaccine-update-your-boss-can-fire-you-if-you-refuse-the-coronavirus-shot.html.

Starks, Briana. "The Double Pandemic: COVID-19 and White Supremacy." *Qualitative Social Work* 20, no. 1–2 (March 2021): 222–224. https://doi.org/10.1177/1473325020986011.

Steyn, Mark. "You Can Laugh - But No One Who Matters Is Laughing." Institute of Public Affairs, April 1, 2015. https://ipa.org.au/ipa-review-articles/you-can-laugh-but-no-one-who-matters-is-laughing.

Taulli, Tom. "How 5G Will Unleash AI." *Forbes*, May 8, 2020. https://www.forbes.com/sites/tomtaulli/2020/05/08/how-5g-will-unleash-ai/?sh=72ad00cb48c3.

Vedmore, Johnny. "Darktrace and Cybereason: The Intelligence Front Companies Seeking to Subjugate the World with the A.I. Singularity." *Unlimited Hangout*, November 3, 2020. https://unlimitedhangout.com/2020/11/reports/darktrace-and-cybereason-the-intelligence-front-companies-seeking-to-subjugate-the-world-with-the-a-i-singularity/.

Vinge, Vernor. "Signs of the Singularity." *IEEE Spectrum* (June 2008). https://andyross.net/singularity.htm.

Zorpette, Glenn. "Waiting for the Rapture." *IEEE Spectrum* (June 2008). https://andyross.net/singularity.htm.

Chapter Five

Andersen, Michael. "Portland Just Passed the Best Low-Density Zoning Reform in US History." Sightline Institute, August 11, 2020. https://www.sightline.org/2020/08/11/on-Wednesday-portland-will-pass-the-best-low-density-zoning-reform-in-us-history/.

Auken, Ida. "This is what 2030 could look like if we win the war on climate change." World Economic Forum, October 31, 2019. https://www.weforum.org/agenda/2019/10/what-happens-if-we-beat-climate-change/.

Azoulay, Audrey. "Towards an Ethics of Artificial Intelligence." *UN Chronicle* 55, no. 4 (January 2019): 24–25. https://doi.org/10.18356/3a8f673a-en.

Burke, Sharon, and Christine Parthemore, eds., *Clout and Climate Change War Game: Participant Briefing Book*, Washington, D.C.: Center for a New American Security, 2008. https://www.files.ethz.ch/isn/100926/2009_06_Clout_and_Climate_Change.pdf.

Calhoun, John B., "Death Squared: The Explosive Growth and Demise of a Mouse Population." *Proceedings of the Royal Society of Medicine* 66, no. 1 Pt 2 (January 1973): 80–8. PMID: 4734760; PMCID: PMC1644264.

Change, Ashley. "New Blueprint Provides Opportunities to Leverage Trillions of Dollars of Global Institutional Investors to Combat Climate Change." The Rockefeller Foundation, September 21, 2021. https://www.rockefellerfoundation.org/news/new-blueprint-provides-opportunities-to-leverage-trillions-of-dollars-of-global-institutional-investors-to-combat-climate-change/.

D'Agostino, Joseph. "The Gates-Buffett Marriage, Designed Not to Bear Fruit." *Population Research Institute*, June 30, 2006. https://archive.pop.org/the-gates-buffett-marriage-designed-not-to-bear-fruit/.

Engelhardt, Marc. "'IOT Improves the Quality of Our Lives.'" Siemens, November 4, 2019. https://new.siemens.com/global/en/company/stories/infrastructure/2019/internet-of-things-interview-with-wef-expert-jeff-merritt.html.

Farley, Sara, and Sara Scherr. "How to reimagine our food systems for a post-COVID world." World Economic Forum, June 9, 2020. https://www.weforum.org/agenda/2020/06/we-need-to-reimagine-our-food-systems-for-a-post-covid-world/.

Fisher, Mary Kate, and Yee San Su. *Food Chain Reaction—A Global Food Security Game.* CAN, 2015. https://www.cna.org/reports/2015/IQR-2015-U-012427.pdf.

Glad, John. *Jewish Eugenics.* Washington, DC: Wooden Shore, 2011.

Government of Canada. *Canada's Implementation of the 2030 Agenda for Sustainable Development: Voluntary National Review.* Ottawa: Global Affairs Canada, 2019. https://sustainabledevelopment.un.org/content/documents/20312Canada_ENGLISH_1 8122_Canadas_Voluntary_National_ReviewENv7.pdf.

"Johnson & Johnson is committed to the Sustainable Development Goals." Janssen, accessed November 15, 2022. https://www.janssen.com/belgium/johnson-johnson-committed-sustainable-development-goals.

Loffredo, Jeremy, and Whitney Webb. "Palantir's Tiberius, Race, and the Public Health Panopticon." *Unlimited Hangout*, December 7, 2020. https://unlimitedhangout.com/2020/12/investigative-series/palantirs-tiberius-race-and-the-public-health-panopticon/.

Marchant, Natalie. "Half of Those Surveyed Are Unaware of the Link between Climate Change and Diseases like COVID-19." World Economic Forum, January 20, 2021. https://www.weforum.org/agenda/2021/01/climate-change-link-infectious-diseases-covid-19-study/.

Miller, John J. "Open the Floodgates." *The Wall Street Journal*, July 7, 2006. https://www.wsj.com/articles/SB115223979105400349.

The MIT Press. "Marina Abramovic's Spirit Cooking." *The MIT Press*, June 28, 2017. https://mitpress.mit.edu/blog/marina-abramovics-spirit-cooking/.

Papachelas, Alexis. "Harari: 'If You Want to Make a Country a Colony, Don't Send the Tanks in. Just Get the Data out.'" ekathimerini.com, October 4, 2020. https://www.ekathimerini.com/opinion/interviews/257687/ljaze-if-you-want-to-make-a-country-a-colony-don-t-send-the-tanks-in-just-get-the-data-out/.

"Population Council." Influence Watch. https://www.influencewatch.org/non-profit/population-council/.

The Rockefeller Foundation. *National COVID-19 Testing Action Plan*. July 2020. https://www.rockefellerfoundation.org/wp-content/uploads/2020/07/TheRockefellerFoundation_TestingEcosystem_7_23.pdf.

Schwab, Klaus. *The Fourth Industrial Revolution*. World Economic Forum, 2016.

"Susan Thompson Buffett Foundation (STBF)." Influence Watch. https://www.influencewatch.org/non-profit/susan-thompson-buffett-foundation/.

Tedeneke, Alem. "World Economic Forum and UN Sign Strategic Partnership Framework." World Economic Forum, June 13, 2019. https://www.weforum.org/press/2019/06/world-economic-forum-and-un-sign-strategic-partnership-framework/.

United Nations Secretary-General. *Roadmap for Financing the 2030 Agenda for Sustainable Development: 2019-2021*. United Nations, July 2019. https://www.un.org/sustainabledevelopment/wp-content/uploads/2019/07/EXEC.SUM_SG-Roadmap-Financing-SDGs-July-2019.pdf.

Winston, Andrew S. "The World in 2030: Nine Megatrends to Watch." *MIT Sloan Management Review*, May 7, 2019. https://sloanreview.mit.edu/article/the-world-in-2030-nine-megatrends-to-watch/.

World Health Organization. *Immunization Agenda 2030: A Global Strategy to Leave No One Behind*. April 2020. https://www.who.int/publications/m/item/immunization-agenda-2030-a-global-strategy-to-leave-no-one-behind.

Chapter Six

Augenbraun, Eliene. "Man becomes human Bitcoin wallet with chip implanted in hand." CBS News, November 14, 2014. https://www.cbsnews.com/news/man-becomes-human-bitcoin-wallet-with-chip-implanted/.

Diego, Raul. "Africa to Become Testing Ground for 'Trust Stamp' Vaccine Record and Payment System." *Mint Press News*, July 10, 2020. https://www.mintpressnews.com/ljaze-trust-stamp-covid-19-vaccine-record-payment-system/269346/.

Fink, Larry. "Larry Fink's Annual 2020 Letter to CEOs." BlackRock, 2020. https://www.blackrock.com/americas-offshore/en/larry-fink-ceo-letter.

Fink, Larry. "Larry Fink's Chairman's Letter to Shareholders." BlackRock, March 24, 2022. https://www.blackrock.com/corporate/investor-relations/larry-fink-chairmans-letter.

Florido, Adrian. "Protests in Sri Lanka Have Turned Violent amid Power, Food and Medicine Shortages." *All Things Considered*, NPR, May 13, 2022. https://www.npr.org/2022/05/13/1098865269/protests-in-sri-lanka-have-turned-violent-amid-power-food-and-medicine-shortages.

Hinchliffe, Tim. "Prepping for a cyber pandemic: Cyber Polygon 2021 to stage supply chain attack simulation." Sociable, February 10, 2021, https://sociable.co/technology/prepping-cyber-pandemic-cyber-polygon-stage-supply-chain-attack-simulation/.

IOSCO Technical Committee. *Regulatory Issues Raised by the Impact of Technological Changes on Market Integrity and Efficiency: Consultation Report.* Madrid: International Organization of Securities Commission, 2011. https://www.iosco.org/library/pubdocs/pdf/IOSCOPD354.pdf.

Kenton, Will. "Dark Pool Liquidity." Investopedia, October 26, 2020. https://www.investopedia.com/terms/d/dark_pool_liquidity.asp.

Middleton, Anna, Mavis Machirori, Jeniffer Mabuka-Maroa, and Tiffany Boughtwood. "We need to talk about big data and genomics. Here's why — and how." World Economic Forum, July 27, 2020. https://www.weforum.org/agenda/2020/07/why-we-need-a-public-conversation-about-big-data-and-genomics/.

"Monaco Digital Advisory Council: A World-Class Team." Extended Monaco, November 2019. https://extendedmonaco.com/en/project/monaco-digital-advisory-council-a-world-class-team/.

Rasheed, Zaheena, and Rathindra Kuruwita. "Sri Lanka Faces 'Man-Made' Food Crisis as Farmers Stop Planting." *Al Jazeera*, May 18, 2022. https://www.aljazeera.com/news/2022/5/18/a-food-crisis-looms-in-sri-lanka-as-farmers-give-up-on-planting.

Raskin, Jamie. "Raskin Restates the Fundamental Importance of the Ukrainian Struggle for National Sovereignty, Democracy and Freedom." Jamie Raskin Press Release, October 25, 2022. https://raskin.house.gov/2022/10/raskin-restates-the-fundamental-importance-of-the-ukrainian-struggle-for-national-sovereignty-democracy-and-freedom.

Tett, Gillian. "Why the US Federal Reserve Turned Again to Blackrock for Help." *Financial Times*, March 26, 2020. https://www.ft.com/content/f3ea07b0-6f5e-11ea-89df-41bea055720b.

Trevelyan, Mark. "Russia forges new partnerships in face of West's 'total hybrid war,' Lavrov says." Reuters, May 14, 2022. https://www.reuters.com/world/lavrov-says-hard-predict-how-long-wests-total-hybrid-war-russia-will-last-2022-05-14/.

Webb, Whitney. "'Charity' Accused of Sex Abuse Coordinating ID2020's Pilot Program for Refugee Newborns." *Unlimited Hangout*, July 29, 2020. https://unlimitedhangout.com/2020/07/reports/charity-accused-of-sex-abuse-coordinating-id2020s-pilot-program-for-refugee-newborns/.

Wigglesworth, Robin. "The ten trillion dollar man: how Larry Fink became king of Wall St." *Financial Times*, October 7, 2021. https://www.ft.com/content/7dfd1e3d-e256-4656-a96d-1204538d75cd.

Wright, Andrew. "How Nanotech Is Changing Your World." World Economic Forum, September 9, 2014. https://www.weforum.org/agenda/2014/09/nanotechnology-revolution-making/.

Conclusion

Baard, Mark. "Sentient world: war games on the grandest scale." *The Register*, June 23, 2007. https://www.theregister.com/2007/06/23/sentient_worlds/?page=1.

Blank, Jim, Daniel Snyder, and David Osen. "Using the Multinational Experiment 4 (MNE4) Modeling and Simulation Federation to Support Joint Experimentation." *Transforming Training and Experimentation through Modelling and Simulation*. Meeting Proceedings RTO-MP-MSG-045, Paper 4, 4.1– 4.14. Neuilly-sur-Seine, France: RTO, 2006.

Blinde, Loren. "NIST seeks AI committee support." Intelligence Community News, August 29, 2022. https://intelligencecommunitynews.com/nist-seeks-ai-committee-support/.

Chaturvedi, Alok. "Computational Challenges for a Sentient World Simulation." Purdue University, March 10, 2006. https://archive.ph/20060911223310/http://www.purdue.edu/acsl/abstract/march10_06.html.

European Council. "An International Treaty on Pandemic Prevention and Preparedness." Consilium, March 25, 2022. https://www.consilium.europa.eu/en/policies/coronavirus/pandemic-treaty/.

Lanese, Nicoletta. "First Human–Monkey Chimeras Developed in China." *The Scientist*, August 5, 2019. https://www.the-scientist.com/news-opinion/first-humanmonkey-chimeras-developed-in-china--66231.

Nikogosian, Haik, and Ilona Kickbusch. "A Pandemic Treaty: Where Are We Now That the Leaders Have Spoken?" *The BMJ*, April 26, 2021. https://blogs.bmj.com/bmj/2021/04/26/a-pandemic-treaty-where-are-we-now-that-the-leaders-have-spoken/.

"Statement of the members of the European Council on COVID-19 and health." European Council, February 25, 2021. https://www.consilium.europa.eu/en/press/press-releases/2021/02/25/statement-of-the-members-of-the-european-council-on-covid-19-and-health-25-february-2021/.